	DATE DUE	
FEB 2 3 2009		JUL 2 4 2009
OCT 1 4 2009		
JUN 1 1 2011		

Prayers for Forgiveness
that Save from the Hellfire

The best of sinners are those
who frequently repent
–Ḥadīth–

الاستغفارات المنقذة من النار

Prayers for Forgiveness

that Save from the Hellfire

SEEKING SPIRITUAL ENLIGHTENMENT
THROUGH SINCERE SUPPLICATION

A Collection of Seventy Prayers for Forgiveness
by ʿAllāma Quṭb al-Dīn al-Ḥanafī from Ḥasan al-Baṣrī
Foreword by Shaykh Husain Abdul Sattar, M.D.

Arabic Text with Facing English Translation
and Transliteration by
ABDUR-RAHMAN IBN YUSUF

White Thread Press
LONDON • SANTA BARBARA

11-08 Amazon 9-

First Edition September 2004
First Reprint January 2005
Second Reprint May 2006
Second Enlarged Edition July 2008

ISBN: (*softcover*) 978-1-933764-07-8
ISBN: (*hardcover*) 978-0-9728358-6-2

Published by:
White Thread Press
California USA
www.whitethreadpress.com
info@whitethreadpress.com

Distributed in the UK by:
Azhar Academy Ltd. London
sales@azharacademy.com

Library of Congress Control Number: 2004104320

Book design and typesetting by ARM
Cover design by Ather Ali
♾ Printed and bound in the United States of America on premium acid-free paper.

For online audio recordings of the seventy prayers for forgiveness please visit
www.whitethreadpress.com/publications/prayers_forgiveness.htm

For My Grandfather Qārī Muhammad and
My Ustādh Mawlānā Abdur Rahim Abu Nu'man,
for their deep inspiration
–Translator–

In the name of Allāh, Most Gracious, Most Merciful.
All praise is for Allāh, Lord of the Worlds, and may peace
and blessings be upon His Messenger Muḥammad,
the Mercy to the Worlds.

Contents

TRANSLITERATION KEY

ء (أ إ)	ʾ (A slight catch in the breath. It is also used to indicate where the *hamza* has been dropped from the beginning of a word.)
ا	a, ā
ب	b
ت	t
ث	th (Should be pronounced as the *th* in *thin* or *thirst*.)
ج	j
ح	ḥ (Tensely breathed *h* sound.)
خ	kh (Pronounced like the *ch* in Scottish *loch* with the mouth hollowed to produce a full sound.)
د	d
ذ	dh (Should be pronounced as the *th* in *this* or *that*.)
ر	r
ز	z
س	s
ش	sh
ص	ṣ (A heavy *s* pronounced far back in the mouth with the mouth hollowed to produce a full sound.)
ض	ḍ (A heavy *d/dh* pronounced far back in the mouth with the mouth hollowed to produce a full sound.)
ط	ṭ (A heavy *t* pronounced far back in the mouth with the mouth hollowed to produce a full sound.)
ظ	ẓ (A heavy *dh* pronounced far back in the mouth with the mouth hollowed to produce a full sound.)
ع	ʿ, ʿa, ʿi, ʿu (Pronounced from the throat.)
غ	gh (Pronounced like a throaty French *r* with the mouth hollowed to produce a full sound.)
ف	f
ق	q (A guttural *q* sound with the mouth hollowed to produce a full sound.)
ك	k
ل	l
م	m
ن	n
و	w, ū, u.
ه	h
ي	y, ī, i
ﷺ	Used following the mention of the Messenger Muḥammad, translated as, “May Allāh bless him and give him peace.”
عليه السلام	Used following the mention of a Prophet or Messenger of Allāh, translated as, “May the peace of Allāh be upon him.”
رضي الله عنه	Used following the mention of a Companion of the Messenger, translated as, “May Allāh be pleased with him.”
رضي الله عنهم	Used following the mention of more than one Companion of the Messenger (and also after a female Companion in this work), translated as, “May Allāh be pleased with them.”

The *duʿās* in this book have been transliterated using a convention different from the standard used for transliterating Arabic terms in the main text. Hence, words are represented as they should be pronounced and the interword connections are transliterated according to the following guidelines:

(1) Silent *hamzas* (*waṣl*) have been omitted and replaced with an apostrophe ('). In this case, the word before it should be connected to the letter after the apostrophe; e.g., *wa 'l-māli.*

(2) Commas have been added to indicate appropriate places of pause. Letters enclosed in parentheses are not read when pausing; e.g., *fī khayr(in).*

(3) In instances where there is elision (*idgham*) between two words, the words are transliterated in their elided forms; e.g., *wāsi-ʿaw wa shifāʾam min.*

Foreword

Reflecting on our deeds in light of Allāh's greatness, one can only wonder how anything we do could ever be worthy of presentation before such an Exalted Being. What could we present to the Owner of all? What could we offer to the One who simply says, "Be," and it is? What could we place before the One whose status is so exalted that it is neither diminished nor strengthened by the quality of what we present? Despite our imperfections, it is only by the infinite mercy of Allāh that we are rewarded for the minute gifts we place before Him.

Casting aside the issue of whether our deeds are worthy of presentation before our Creator, the reality is that each of us carries a load of sin and disobedience upon our shoulders. By design we are imperfect creatures prone to making mistakes. The Prophet ﷺ said, "Every descendent of Adam is a sinner, and the best of the sinners are those who frequently repent" (*Tirmidhī*).

The mercy of Allāh is so greatly infinite and His position so grand, that rather than immediately punishing us, He has granted us a grace period in which to seek forgiveness for our sins. And as if that were not enough, Allāh then gave us the means by which to wipe away our sins and their negative effects. These are called supplications of forgiveness (*istighfārāt*).

Perhaps the simplest form of *istighfār* is to reflect on our daily routine and to seek forgiveness for the errors that are apparent. This was the *Sunna* of the Prophet ﷺ and has been the way of the righteous who follow in his footsteps. However, just as with any art, time spent in the company of those who are deep in their repentance provides an apprenticeship in how to sincerely turn with a lowered head toward our Sustainer.

A pious scholar from the past was once asked what we should do to rectify our connection with our Lord. He said, "Seek the company of the righteous." He was then asked, "What if the righteous are no longer present among us?" He replied, "Read their books."

It is through the mercy of Allāh that the work present in your hands is such a book. This text contains a collection of prayers as transmitted from the great scholar Ḥasan al-Baṣrī. Reading through these supplications lends the seeker an opportunity to realize how our righteous predecessors viewed their actions and deeds when standing before Allāh. It is my hope that the publication of this text by my close friend Muftī Abdur-Rahman will guide those who desire nearness to Allāh on how to lower themselves before their Sustainer.

The process of *istighfār* goes hand in hand with deep self-reflection. We do not consider seeking forgiveness for a misdeed unless we see the act as a sin. Perhaps such a lack of insight is the greatest tribulation of our time. I pray that Allāh opens our eyes to the reality of His grandeur, the reality of our servitude, and the power of returning to Him.

Husain Abdul Sattar
Sunday, February 29, 2004

Introduction

In the present age of computers and technological gadgetry, it is generally considered a good practice to routinely clear unused and temporary files from one's computer. This keeps the machine running smoothly and decreases the chances of malfunction and crashing. Similarly, we delete unimportant messages from our e-mail inboxes to keep them uncluttered and open to receiving new incoming messages.

Though we spend time routinely cleaning up our machines, we often do so while neglecting our hearts, which are far more worthy of our careful attention since they become spiritually malnourished and deadened by the overwhelming burden of sin. The Companion Abū Hurayra ﵁ relates that the Messenger of Allāh ﷺ said, "When a believer commits a sin, a black dot appears on his heart. If he repents and seeks forgiveness, his heart becomes purified. If he advances in sin, the black dots increase until they overcome his heart. These black dots constitute the encrusted pollution (*ra'n*) that God Almighty refers to in the verse: 'No, indeed! But, encrusted over their hearts is what they have earned.'" (Qur'ān 83:14) (*Tirmidhī*).

If one allows sins to accumulate on his or her heart in the form of this inner rust, the heart gradually becomes blind and unreceptive to spiritual realities. One can easily observe this inner lack of spiritual cognition when, for example, a person yawns at the mention of the Hellfire and its severity, whereas another faints upon hearing of the same. We are thus in need of a reliable method and rigid routine for cleansing our hearts of the pollution they accumulate from frequent sinning.

Cleansing the heart is achieved through the remembrance of Allāh (*dhikr*), repentance (*tawba*), seeking forgiveness (*istighfār*), and humbly turning to Him in penitence (*ināba*). The Messenger of Allāh ﷺ did this seventy to a hundred times a day, despite being inerrant and guarded from sin (*maʿṣūm*). He ﷺ also said, "Every descendant of Adam is a sinner, and the best of the sinners are those who repent" (*Sunan al-Tirmidhī*). When a person makes sincere repentance (*tawba naṣūḥ*) for his sins, no matter how severe they may be, Allāh purifies his heart and treats him as if he never committed them.

Why is it such a bounty that we are able to turn to the Almighty and seek His forgiveness? Turning to Allāh in repentance and seeking His forgiveness provide us the release we need when feeling overwhelmed by the burden of sin. They give us a way out, another chance, a sense of lightheartedness, hope, and inspiration needed to turn a new page in life and start afresh. It is through forgiveness that we gain so much hope in our religion that there remains no reason whatsoever for us to despair of Allāh's mercy. Allāh advises us not to run away from Him in fear but to run toward Him like a baby running into its mother's lap. So lovingly does Almighty Allāh address His sinful servants: "Say (to humanity, O Muḥammad): O My servants—those (of you) who have committed (sins in great) excess against their own souls—never despair of the mercy of Allāh! For, indeed, Allāh forgives sins, one and all. Indeed, it is He who is the All-Forgiving, the Mercy-Giving. So turn in penitence to your Lord. And submit yourselves to Him" (Qur'ān 39:53–54).

Many want to seek forgiveness and cherish the thought of being purified, but do not know how to embark on this path. For instance, they do not know what words to use or what to seek forgiveness for; or they have forgotten about many of the sins they have committed or perhaps deem many of them trivial and insignificant; or they think there is no need to seek forgiveness. And if they do seek forgiveness, they do so only superficially, using generalities like "O Allāh, forgive all my sins" or "Forgive them if You wish"; they do so without any vigor or persistence. The Messenger of Allāh ﷺ said, "When one of you asks Allāh, . . . he should ask earnestly, for Allāh does as He wishes and there is none to compel Him" (*Bukhārī*).

THE OBJECTIVE OF THIS BOOK

The most superior prayers for seeking forgiveness (*istighfārāt*) are those mentioned in the Qur'ān, followed by those related from the Messenger of Allāh ﷺ. There can be nothing superior to what has come from these two sacred sources. These prayers are found in many of the popular prayer collections. Thereafter, we may also benefit from the prayers and invocations passed down by our pious predecessors, who were well informed of the subtle ways of how to ask Allāh and what to ask for.

Among these spiritual luminaries was Ḥasan al-Baṣrī (may Allāh be pleased with him), to whom the seventy prayers for forgiveness in this book (along with a few concluding prayers) are attributed. ʿAllāma Quṭb al-Dīn al-Ḥanafī transmitted them from Ḥasan al-Baṣrī in his *Kitāb Adʿiyat al-Ḥajj wa 'l-ʿUmra* (Book of Prayers of Ḥajj and ʿUmra) and referred to them as *Al-Istighfārāt al-Munqidha min al-Nār* (Prayers for Forgiveness that Save from the Hellfire). Although originally suggested for reading on the seventh, ninth, and tenth of Dhū 'l-Ḥijja, these prayers are worthy of being read every day because they encompass most of what a person needs to seek forgiveness for.

Popular prayer litanies, such as Mullā ʿAlī al-Qārī's *Al-Ḥizb al-Aʿẓam* (The Great Litany) and Shaykh ʿAbdullāh ʿAlawī al-Ḥaddād's collection, contain various prayers for forgiveness. However, there are very few litanies available entirely dedicated to such prayers. Hence, this collection of *istighfārāt* is intended for use alongside other general litanies that one may regularly recite.

HOW TO READ THIS LITANY

One should try to read all seventy prayers every day (in addition to other prayers that one is in the habit of reading), in order to fulfill the practice of the Messenger ﷺ, who said, "By Allāh, I seek forgiveness from Allāh and repent to Him more than seventy times each day" (*Bukhārī*). If one is unable to do this, he or she may read ten prayers each day to complete all seventy over seven days. Otherwise one may read any number that one can. The Urdu translation of this collection, by Mawlānā Muḥammad Ḥamīd ʿAbd al-Majīd (may Allāh bless him—for his work introduced me to this beautiful litany), has been arranged in seven sections: ten prayers for each day of the week.

The most important part of any prayer for forgiveness is that the suppliant focus on what he or she is saying, reflect on the meaning, and then allow the words to flow from the heart. One should feel remorseful and regretful over one's sins, express an earnest desire to be forgiven, and promise never again to commit such sins intentionally. Otherwise, one's invocation may be an empty reading of words.

THE LAYOUT OF THIS BOOK

The Arabic text of this edition is based on published versions of ʿAllāma Quṭb al-Dīn al-Ḥanafī's *Kitāb Adʿiyat al-Ḥajj wa 'l-ʿUmra* and on the Arabic text of Mawlānā ʿAbd al-Majīd's Urdu translation. It is completely vowelled and set in clear and legible script. A transliteration is also provided for those unable to read Arabic. Although one may use the transliterated text, learning to read Arabic from a qualified teacher is strongly encouraged. The English translation is set on the facing pages so as not to disrupt fluid reading of the Arabic for those who choose not to refer to the translation. The chain of transmission (*sanad*) from ʿAllāma Quṭb al-Dīn al-Ḥanafī to Ḥasan al-Baṣrī of the seventy prayers and biographical notes on ʿAllāma Quṭb al-Dīn can be found at the back of the book.

Divine guidance and success (*tawfīq*) is only from Allāh. I am grateful to Allāh for granting me the ability to prepare this work for the English-speaking world and present these noble prayers set before you. I pray that Allāh make this work a cause of forgiveness for myself, my family, my teachers, and all those who assisted in its publication (whether they were aware of it or not), for I do not have much else to put my hopes in to be saved from the Hellfire on the Day of Judgment. My simple request to all who derive benefit from this work is to pray that Allāh accept me for the service of His *dīn* in spite of my immense shortcomings. *Āmīn.*

Abdur-Rahman ibn Yusuf Mangera
Muḥarram 10, 1425 | March 2, 2004

الاستغفارات المنقذة من النار

Prayers for Forgiveness

that Save from the Hellfire

(1) O Allāh, I seek Your forgiveness for every sin that my body, empowered by the good health that You had granted, was able to commit; every sin that came within the reaches of my power only due to the grace of Your bounties; every sin to which my hand, nourished by Your ample sustenance, extended. And while sinning, I hid myself behind Your veil from the people; and when fearing You, while engrossed in my sin, I relied on Your assurance of safety and forgiveness; and I took refuge in You, with Your clemency, not to smite me, and I depended on You, with Your noble countenance and pardon, to forgive me.

So send blessings and peace, O my Lord, upon our Master Muḥammad, and upon the family of our Master Muḥammad, and forgive my sin, O Best of those who forgive!

Note: This ending prayer follows each one of the seventy prayers in the actual litany but has only been mentioned once in this translated edition.

(2) O Allāh, I seek Your forgiveness for every sin that invites me to Your anger, or draws me near Your displeasure, or makes me inclined to that which You have prohibited, or distances me from [the bliss and success] to which You have invited me.

﴿١﴾ اَللّٰهُمَّ إِنِّيْ أَسْتَغْفِرُكَ لِكُلِّ ذَنْبٍ قَوِيَ عَلَيْهِ بَدَنِيْ بِعَافِيَتِكَ، وَنَالَتْهُ قُدْرَتِيْ بِفَضْلِ نِعْمَتِكَ، وَانْبَسَطَتْ إِلَيْهِ يَدِيْ بِسِعَةِ رِزْقِكَ، وَاحْتَجَبْتُ عَنِ النَّاسِ بِسِتْرِكَ، وَاتَّكَلْتُ فِيْهِ عِنْدَ خَوْفِيْ مِنْكَ عَلٰى أَمَانِكَ، وَوَثِقْتُ مِنْ سَطْوَتِكَ عَلَيَّ فِيْهِ بِحِلْمِكَ، وَعَوَّلْتُ فِيْهِ عَلٰى كَرَمِ وَجْهِكَ وَعَفْوِكَ ❁

فَصَلِّ يَا رَبِّ وَسَلِّمْ وَبَارِكْ عَلٰى سَيِّدِنَا مُحَمَّدٍ وَّعَلٰى آلِ سَيِّدِنَا مُحَمَّدٍ وَّاغْفِرْهُ لِيْ يَا خَيْرَ الْغَافِرِيْنَ ❁

﴿٢﴾ اَللّٰهُمَّ إِنِّيْ أَسْتَغْفِرُكَ لِكُلِّ ذَنْبٍ يَّدْعُوْ إِلٰى غَضَبِكَ، أَوْ يُدْنِيْ مِنْ سَخَطِكَ، أَوْ يَمِيْلُ بِيْ إِلٰى مَا نَهَيْتَنِيْ عَنْهُ، أَوْ يُبَاعِدُنِيْ عَمَّا دَعَوْتَنِيْ إِلَيْهِ ❁

(3) O Allāh, I seek Your forgiveness for every sin into which I, in my deviance, lured one of Your creation, or which I, with my cunning, deceived him into doing—hence teaching him such wicked deeds that he was previously unaware of, and making attractive to him those that he was aware of. Now I am to meet You tomorrow, with my burden of sins along with the burdens of others' sins.

(4) O Allāh, I seek Your forgiveness for every sin that calls to deviance; for every sin that leads from the path of guidance; for every sin that diminishes abundant wealth; for every sin that obliterates long-possessed property and inherited family wealth; for every sin that deprives me of honorable repute; and for every sin that drives away my friends and family.

(5) O Allāh, I seek Your forgiveness for every sin in which I exhausted my limbs, by day and by night—all the while keeping myself hidden, out of shame from Your servants, with Your covering over me; and indeed, there is nothing to cover my sins but what You cover me with.

(6) O Allāh, I seek Your forgiveness for every sin with which my enemies intended to disgrace me, but You turned their plotting away from me and did not assist them in disgracing me, as though

﴿٣﴾ اَللّٰهُمَّ إِنِّيْ أَسْتَغْفِرُكَ لِكُلِّ ذَنْبٍ أَسْلَمْتُ إِلَيْهِ أَحَدًا مِّنْ خَلْقِكَ بِغَوَايَتِيْ، أَوْ خَدَعْتُهُ بِحِيْلَتِيْ، فَعَلَّمْتُهُ مِنْهُ مَا جَهِلَ، وَزَيَّنْتُ لَهُ مَا قَدْ عَلِمَ، وَلَقِيْتُكَ غَدًا بِأَوْزَارِيْ وَأَوْزَارٍ مَّعَ أَوْزَارِيْ ❁

﴿٤﴾ اَللّٰهُمَّ إِنِّيْ أَسْتَغْفِرُكَ لِكُلِّ ذَنْبٍ يَّدْعُوْ إِلَى الْغَيِّ، وَيُضِلُّ عَنِ الرُّشْدِ، وَيُقِلُّ الْوَفْرَ، وَيَمْحَقُ التَّالِدَةَ، وَيُخْمِلُ الذِّكْرَ، وَيُقِلُّ الْعَدَدَ ❁

﴿٥﴾ اَللّٰهُمَّ إِنِّيْ أَسْتَغْفِرُكَ لِكُلِّ ذَنْبٍ أَتْعَبْتُ فِيْهِ جَوَارِحِيْ فِيْ لَيْلِيْ وَنَهَارِيْ، وَقَدِ اسْتَتَرْتُ حَيَاءً مِّنْ عِبَادِكَ بِسِتْرِكَ، وَلَا سِتْرَ إِلَّا مَا سَتَرْتَنِيْ بِهِ ❁

﴿٦﴾ اَللّٰهُمَّ إِنِّيْ أَسْتَغْفِرُكَ لِكُلِّ ذَنْبٍ قَصَدَنِيْ بِهِ أَعْدَائِيْ لِهَتْكِيْ، فَصَرَفْتَ كَيْدَهُمْ عَنِّيْ، وَلَمْ تُعِنْهُمْ عَلٰى فَضِيْحَتِيْ كَأَنِّيْ لَكَ مُطِيْعٌ،

I were Your obedient servant; and You sustained me until it seemed as though I were Your friend. Until when, O my Lord, will I disobey You and You continue giving me respite? Long indeed have I disobeyed You and You have not punished me; and long indeed have I, with all my evil deeds, beseeched You and You have granted me my requests. What meager thanks of mine can measure up, in Your sight, to even one of Your many blessings upon me?

(7) O Allāh, I seek Your forgiveness for every sin for which I presented my repentance before You; and regarding which I stood before You swearing an oath in Your name and called Your friends from among Your servants to be my witnesses—that I would never return to disobeying You. But when Satan with his cunning tempted me to return to it; and Your forsaking me [due to Your anger over my impiety] caused me to [despairingly] waver toward it; and my lower self invited me to disobey You once more; I hid myself in shame from Your servants, but openly and daringly committed sins before You, though I knew full well that no covering nor any closed door could conceal me from You and no veil could hide me from Your sight. I still defied You by disobediently doing what You had prohibited to me; but [despite my iniquity], You did not remove Your covering from me, but treated me equal to Your pious servants, as though I had always

وَّنَصَرْتَنِيْ حَتّٰى كَأَنِّيْ لَكَ وَلِيٌّ، وَإِلٰى مَتٰى يَا رَبِّ أَعْصِيْ فَتُمْهِلُنِيْ؟ وَطَالَمَا عَصَيْتُكَ فَلَمْ تُؤَاخِذْنِيْ، وَسَأَلْتُكَ عَلٰى سُوْءِ فِعْلِيْ فَأَعْطَيْتَنِيْ، فَأَيُّ شُكْرٍ يَّقُوْمُ عِنْدَكَ بِنِعْمَةٍ مِّنْ نِّعَمِكَ عَلَيَّ؟ ❁

﴿٧﴾ اَللّٰهُمَّ إِنِّيْ أَسْتَغْفِرُكَ لِكُلِّ ذَنْبٍ قَدَّمْتُ إِلَيْكَ تَوْبَتِيْ مِنْهُ، وَوَاجَهْتُكَ بِقَسَمِيْ بِكَ، وَأَشْهَدتُّ عَلٰى نَفْسِيْ بِذٰلِكَ أَوْلِيَائَكَ مِنْ عِبَادِكَ أَنِّيْ غَيْرُ عَائِدٍ إِلٰى مَعْصِيَتِكَ، فَلَمَّا قَصَدَنِيْ إِلَيْهِ بِكَيْدِهِ الشَّيْطَانُ، وَمَالَ بِيْ إِلَيْهِ الْخُذْلَانُ، وَدَعَتْنِيْ نَفْسِيْ إِلَى الْعِصْيَانِ، اسْتَتَرْتُ حَيَاءً مِّنْ عِبَادِكَ جَرَاءَةً مِّنِّيْ عَلَيْكَ، وَأَنَا أَعْلَمُ أَنَّهُ لَا يُكِنُّنِيْ مِنْكَ سِتْرٌ وَّلَا بَابٌ، وَّلَا يَحْجُبُ نَظَرَكَ حِجَابٌ، فَخَالَفْتُكَ فِي الْمَعْصِيَةِ إِلٰى مَا نَهَيْتَنِيْ عَنْهُ، ثُمَّ مَا كَشَفْتَ السِّتْرَ، وَسَاوَيْتَنِيْ بِأَوْلِيَائِكَ، كَأَنِّيْ لَا أَزَالُ لَكَ مُطِيْعًا وَّإِلٰى أَمْرِكَ مُسْرِعًا وَّمِنْ وَّعِيْدِكَ فَازِعًا، فَلَبِسْتُ عَلٰى عِبَادِكَ

been an obedient servant and swift to fulfill Your every command and fearful of Your warnings. I remained obscure in front of Your servants, and none besides You knew my secret. You did not single me out from Your servants with a mark of disgrace, but showered upon me blessings like theirs; and with this You distinguished me over them as though I were, in Your sight, of a status like theirs. All this was owing only of Your forbearance and abundant blessings—generous grace from You to me. For You then, O my Lord, belongs all praise. I ask from You, O Allāh, just as You have covered my evil deeds in this world, that You not humiliate me with them on the Day of Judgment. [Forgive my sins,] O Most Merciful of the merciful!

(8) O Allāh, I seek Your forgiveness for every sin for which I spent the night in sleeplessness, savoring the pleasure of soon committing it and waiting in eager anticipation of its realization and fulfillment—until when morning came, I presented myself before You in the guise of the pious, while concealing in my heart what was against Your pleasure. [Forgive me,] O Lord of the Worlds!

(9) O Allāh, I seek Your forgiveness for every sin by which I wronged one of Your friends and assisted one of Your enemies;

وَلَا يَعْلَمُ سَرِيْرَتِيْ غَيْرُكَ، فَلَمْ تَسِمْنِيْ بِغَيْرِ سِمَتِهِمْ، بَلْ أَسْبَغْتَ عَلَيَّ مِثْلَ نِعْمَتِهِمْ، ثُمَّ فَضَّلْتَنِيْ بِذٰلِكَ عَلَيْهِم كَأَنِّيْ عِنْدَكَ فِيْ دَرَجَتِهِمْ، وَمَا ذَاكَ إِلَّا لِحِلْمِكَ وَفَضْلِ نِعْمَتِكَ فَضْلًا مِّنْكَ عَلَيَّ، فَلَكَ الْحَمْدُ يَا مَوْلَايَ، فَأَسْأَلُكَ يَا اَللهُ كَمَا سَتَرْتَهُ عَلَيَّ فِي الدُّنْيَا أَن لَّا تَفْضَحَنِيْ بِهِ يَوْمَ الْقِيَامَةِ، يَا أَرْحَمَ الرَّاحِمِيْنَ ❁

﴿٨﴾ اَللّٰهُمَّ إِنِّيْ أَسْتَغْفِرُكَ لِكُلِّ ذَنْبٍ سَهِرْتُ فِيْهِ لَيْلَتِيْ فِيْ لَذَّتِيْ فِي التَّأَنِّيْ لِإِتْيَانِهِ، وَالتَّخَلُّصِ إِلٰى وُجُوْدِهِ وَتَحْصِيْلِهِ، حَتّٰى إِذَا أَصْبَحْتُ حَضَرْتُ إِلَيْكَ بِحِلْيَةِ الصَّالِحِيْنَ، وَأَنَا مُضْمِرٌ خِلَافَ رِضَاكَ، يَا رَبَّ الْعَالَمِيْنَ ❁

﴿٩﴾ اَللّٰهُمَّ إِنِّيْ أَسْتَغْفِرُكَ لِكُلِّ ذَنْبٍ ظَلَمْتُ بِسَبَبِهِ وَلِيًّا مِّنْ أَوْلِيَائِكَ،

or of which I spoke favorably, against Your liking, or upon which I rode away from Your obedience; or to which I advanced in open defiance of Your command.

(10) O Allāh, I seek Your forgiveness for every sin that breeds rancor, for every sin that causes calamity to strike, for every sin that makes my enemies to rejoice at my misfortune, for every sin that removes the coverings [from my faults and the faults of others], and for every sin that withholds rain from the heavens.

(11) O Allāh, I seek Your forgiveness for every sin that diverted me from the way to which You had guided me; or from doing what You had commanded me and avoiding what You had forbidden me; or from doing anything to which You had directed me, in which there would have been for me prosperity and attainment of Your pleasure, Your love, and Your nearness.

(12) O Allāh, I seek Your forgiveness for every sin that I forgot but You recorded; that I made little of but You noted; that I openly committed but You quietly concealed—and if I were to repent to You for it, You would surely forgive it.

وَنَصَرْتُ بِهِۦ عَدُوًّا مِّنْ أَعْدَائِكَ، أَوْ تَكَلَّمْتُ فِيْهِ لِغَيْرِ مَحَبَّتِكَ، أَوْ نَهَضْتُ فِيْهِ إِلَىٰ غَيْرِ طَاعَتِكَ، أَوْ ذَهَبْتُ فِيْهِ إِلَىٰ غَيْرِ أَمْرِكَ ❁

﴿١٠﴾ اَللّٰهُمَّ إِنِّيْ أَسْتَغْفِرُكَ لِكُلِّ ذَنْبٍ يُّوْرِثُ الضَّغْنَاءَ، وَيُحِلُّ الْبَلَاءَ، وَيُشْمِتُ الْأَعْدَاءَ، وَيَكْشِفُ الْغِطَاءَ، وَيَحْبِسُ الْقَطْرَ مِنَ السَّمَاءِ ❁

﴿١١﴾ اَللّٰهُمَّ إِنِّيْ أَسْتَغْفِرُكَ لِكُلِّ ذَنْبٍ أَلْهَانِيْ عَمَّا هَدَيْتَنِيْ إِلَيْهِ، وَأَمَرْتَنِيْ بِهِۦ أَوْ نَهَيْتَنِيْ عَنْهُ، أَوْ دَلَلْتَنِيْ عَلَيْهِ مِمَّا فِيْهِ الْحَظُّ لِيْ، وَالْبُلُوْغُ إِلَىٰ رِضَاكَ وَاتِّبَاعُ مَحَبَّتِكَ وَإِيْثَارُ الْقُرْبِ مِنْكَ ❁

﴿١٢﴾ اَللّٰهُمَّ إِنِّيْ أَسْتَغْفِرُكَ لِكُلِّ ذَنْبٍ نَّسِيْتُهُۥ فَأَحْصَيْتَهُۥ، وَتَهَاوَنْتُ بِهِۦ فَأَثْبَتَّهُۥ، وَجَاهَرْتُكَ بِهِۦ فَسَتَرْتَهُۥ عَلَيَّ، وَلَوْ تُبْتُ إِلَيْكَ مِنْهُ لَغَفَرْتَهُۥ ❁

(13) O Allāh, I seek Your forgiveness for every sin for which, even before its completion, I anticipated Your swift punishment, but You granted me respite and draped over me a covering, yet I spared no effort in trying to tear it away from myself.

(14) O Allāh, I seek Your forgiveness for every sin that You prohibited to me but I opposed You by committing; and every sin that You forewarned me of but I remained firm in committing; and every sin that You deemed abominable but my lower self made attractive to me.

(15) O Allāh, I seek Your forgiveness for every sin that turns away from me Your mercy, or causes Your vengeance to befall me, or deprives me of Your generosity, or takes away from me Your blessings.

(16) O Allāh, I seek Your forgiveness for every sin that I reproached or condemned one of Your creation for committing, but then myself plunged into and brazenly committed before You.

﴿١٣﴾ اَللّٰهُمَّ إِنِّيْ أَسْتَغْفِرُكَ لِكُلِّ ذَنْبٍ تَوَقَّعْتُ مِنكَ قَبْلَ انْقِضَائِهٖ تَعْجِيلَ الْعُقُوْبَةِ، فَأَمْهَلْتَنِيْ وَأَسْبَلْتَ عَلَيَّ سِتْرًا، فَلَمْ آلُ فِيْ هَتْكِهٖ عَنِّيْ جُهْدًا ❁

﴿١٤﴾ اَللّٰهُمَّ إِنِّيْ أَسْتَغْفِرُكَ لِكُلِّ ذَنْبٍ نَّهَيْتَنِيْ عَنْهُ فَخَالَفْتُكَ إِلَيْهِ، وَحَذَّرْتَنِيْ إِيَّاهُ فَأَقَمْتُ عَلَيْهِ، وَقَبَّحْتَهُ عَلَيَّ فَزَيَّنَتْهُ لِيْ نَفْسِيْ ❁

﴿١٥﴾ اَللّٰهُمَّ إِنِّيْ أَسْتَغْفِرُكَ لِكُلِّ ذَنْبٍ يَّصْرِفُ عَنِّيْ رَحْمَتَكَ، أَوْ يُحِلُّ بِيْ نِقْمَتَكَ، أَوْ يَحْرِمُنِيْ كَرَامَتَكَ، أَوْ يُزِيْلُ عَنِّيْ نِعْمَتَكَ ❁

﴿١٦﴾ اَللّٰهُمَّ إِنِّيْ أَسْتَغْفِرُكَ لِكُلِّ ذَنْبٍ عَيَّرْتُ بِهٖ أَحَدًا مِّنْ خَلْقِكَ، أَوْ قَبَّحْتُ مِنْ فِعْلِ أَحَدٍ مِّنْ بَرِيَّتِكَ، ثُمَّ تَقَحَّمْتُ عَلَيْهِ وَانْتَهَكْتُهُ جَرَاءَةً مِّنِّيْ عَلَيْكَ ❁

(17) O Allāh, I seek Your forgiveness for every sin for which I repented to You and then embarked on committing again; but then I felt ashamed before You and fearful of You while engrossed in it, so I invoked Your forgiveness for it once more, but [in my weakness] returned to it yet again.

(18) O Allāh, I seek Your forgiveness for every sin that overtook me and became unavoidable for me when I took a covenant with You, or made a promise to You, or took an oath by You in regard to a responsibility to one of Your creation, and then I broke it without any excuse; it was in fact my arrogance that made me step down from fulfilling it and my insolence that made me reject observing it.

(19) O Allāh, I seek Your forgiveness for every sin that overcame me [when I abused] a bounty You had bestowed upon me, using it to embolden myself in disobeying You, opposing Your command, and insolently advancing toward sin despite Your warnings [of punishment].

(20) O Allāh, I seek Your forgiveness for every sin in which I gave preference to my base desire over Your obedience and my passion

﴿١٧﴾ اَللّٰهُمَّ إِنِّيْ أَسْتَغْفِرُكَ لِكُلِّ ذَنْبٍ تُبْتُ إِلَيْكَ مِنْهُ وَأَقْدَمْتُ عَلٰى فِعْلِهِ، فَاسْتَحْيَيْتُ مِنكَ وَأَنَا عَلَيْهِ، وَرَهِبْتُكَ وَأَنَا فِيْهِ، ثُمَّ اسْتَقَلْتُكَ مِنْهُ وَعُدتُّ إِلَيْهِ ❁

﴿١٨﴾ اَللّٰهُمَّ إِنِّيْ أَسْتَغْفِرُكَ لِكُلِّ ذَنْبٍ تَوَرَّكَ عَلَيَّ وَوَجَبَ فِيْ شَيْءٍ فَعَلْتُهُ، بِسَبَبِ عَهْدٍ عَهِدتُّكَ عَلَيْهِ، أَوْ عَقْدٍ عَقَدتُّهُ لَكَ، أَوْ ذِمَّةٍ آلَيْتُ بِهَا مِنْ أَجْلِكَ لِأَحَدٍ مِّنْ خَلْقِكَ، ثُمَّ نَقَضْتُ ذٰلِكَ مِنْ غَيْرِ ضَرُوْرَةٍ لَّزِمَتْنِي فِيْهِ، بَلِ اسْتَنْزَلَنِيْ عَنِ الْوَفَاءِ بِهِ الْبَطَرُ، وَأَسْخَطَنِيْ عَن رِّعَايَتِهِ الْأَشَرُ ❁

﴿١٩﴾ اَللّٰهُمَّ إِنِّيْ أَسْتَغْفِرُكَ لِكُلِّ ذَنْبٍ لَّحِقَنِيْ بِسَبَبِ نِعْمَةٍ أَنْعَمْتَ بِهَا عَلَيَّ، فَتَقَوَّيْتُ بِهَا عَلٰى مَعَاصِيْكَ، وخَالَفْتُ فِيْهَا أَمْرَكَ، وَأَقْدَمْتُ بِهَا عَلٰى وَعِيْدِكَ ❁

﴿٢٠﴾ اَللّٰهُمَّ إِنِّيْ أَسْتَغْفِرُكَ لِكُلِّ ذَنْبٍ قَدَّمْتُ فِيْهِ شَهْوَتِيْ عَلٰى

over Your command—thus I contented myself with Your wrath and subjected myself to Your displeasure, though You had forbidden me, presented Your admonition to me, and established the proof of it to me through Your warnings [of punishment in Your revelations]. I seek Your forgiveness, O Allāh, and repent to You.

(21) O Allāh, I seek Your forgiveness for every sin that I knew myself to have committed, then forgot about or remembered, or that I had committed intentionally or unintentionally; and I have no doubt that it is a sin about which You will question me and for which my soul is held captive to You, even if I have become forgetful and heedless of it.

(22) O Allāh, I seek Your forgiveness for every sin that I committed in front of You knowing full well that You were watching me. I intended to turn to You in repentance for it, but I was made to forget to invoke Your forgiveness—it was Satan that made me forget.

(23) O Allāh, I seek Your forgiveness for every sin upon which I embarked, thinking well of You—that You would forgive me for

طَاعَتِكَ، وَآثَرْتُ فِيْهِ مَحَبَّتِي عَلَى أَمْرِكَ، فَأَرْضَيْتُ نَفْسِيْ بِغَضَبِكَ، وَعَرَّضْتُهَا لِسَخَطِكَ، إِذْ نَهَيْتَنِيْ وَقَدَّمْتَ إِلَيَّ فِيْهِ إِنْذَارَكَ وَتَحَجَّجْتَ عَلَيَّ فِيْهِ بِوَعِيْدِكَ، وَأَسْتَغْفِرُكَ اللَّهُمَّ وَأَتُوْبُ إِلَيْكَ ❁

﴿٢١﴾ اَللَّهُمَّ إِنِّيْ أَسْتَغْفِرُكَ لِكُلِّ ذَنْبٍ عَلِمْتُهُ مِن نَّفْسِيْ فَأَنْسَيْتُهُ، أَوْ ذَكَرْتُهُ، أَوْ تَعَمَّدْتُهُ، أَوْ أَخْطَأْتُ فِيْهِ، وَهُوَ مِمَّا لَا أَشُكُّ أَنَّكَ مُسَائِلِيْ عَنْهُ، وَأَنَّ نَفْسِيْ بِهِ مُرْتَهِنَةٌ لَّدَيْكَ، وَإِنْ كُنْتُ قَدْ نَسِيْتُهُ، وَغَفَلَتْ عَنْهُ نَفْسِيْ ❁

﴿٢٢﴾ اَللَّهُمَّ إِنِّيْ أَسْتَغْفِرُكَ لِكُلِّ ذَنْبٍ وَّاجَهْتُكَ فِيْهِ وَقَدْ أَيْقَنْتُ أَنَّكَ تَرَانِيْ عَلَيْهِ، فَنَوَيْتُ أَنْ أَتُوْبَ إِلَيْكَ مِنْهُ، وَأُنْسِيْتُ أَنْ أَسْتَغْفِرَكَ مِنْهُ، أَنْسَانِيْهِ الشَّيْطَانُ ❁

﴿٢٣﴾ اَللَّهُمَّ إِنِّيْ أَسْتَغْفِرُكَ لِكُلِّ ذَنْبٍ دَخَلْتُ فِيْهِ بِحُسْنِ ظَنِّيْ فِيْكَ

it and not punish me. I thus audaciously continued in committing it while relying, with my knowledge of Your generosity, on You not to disgrace me after having concealed it for me.

(24) O Allāh, I seek Your forgiveness for every sin by which I deserved rejection of my prayers, and refusal of their acceptance, and failure in my hopes being fulfilled, and severance of hope in Your mercy.

(25) O Allāh, I seek Your forgiveness for every sin that brings about illnesses and emaciating diseases, and warrants punishments and misery, and will be a cause of grief and remorse on Judgment Day.

(26) O Allāh, I seek Your forgiveness for every sin that leaves grief on its heel, that causes remorse, that holds back sustenance, and that prevents acceptance of [my] prayers.

(27) O Allāh, I seek Your forgiveness for every sin that I praised with my tongue, or that I resolved upon in my heart, or that my soul took pleasure in, or that my tongue endorsed, or that I effected with my actions, or that I wrote with my hand, or that I committed in any way or caused one of Your servants to commit.

أَنَّكَ لَا تُعَذِّبُنِيْ عَلَيْهِ، وَرَجَوْتُكَ لِمَغْفِرَتِهٖ فَأَقْدَمْتُ عَلَيْهِ، وَقَدْ عَوَّلْتُ نَفْسِيْ عَلٰى مَعْرِفَتِيْ بِكَرَمِكَ أَنْ لَّا تَفْضَحَنِيْ بِهٖ بَعْدَ إِذْ سَتَرْتَهٗ عَلَيَّ ❁

﴿٢٤﴾ اَللّٰهُمَّ إِنِّيْ أَسْتَغْفِرُكَ لِكُلِّ ذَنْبٍ اسْتَوْجَبْتُ بِهٖ مِنْكَ رَدَّ الدُّعَاءِ، وَحِرْمَانَ الْإِجَابَةِ، وَخَيْبَةَ الطَّمَعِ، وَانْقِطَاعَ الرَّجَاءِ ❁

﴿٢٥﴾ اَللّٰهُمَّ إِنِّيْ أَسْتَغْفِرُكَ لِكُلِّ ذَنْبٍ يُّوْرِثُ الْأَسْقَامَ وَالضِّنٰى، وَيُوْجِبُ النِّقَمَ وَالْبَلَاءَ، وَيَكُوْنُ يَوْمَ الْقِيَامَةِ حَسْرَةً وَّنَدَامَةً ❁

﴿٢٦﴾ اَللّٰهُمَّ إِنِّيْ أَسْتَغْفِرُكَ لِكُلِّ ذَنْبٍ يُّعَقِّبُ الْحَسْرَةَ، وَيُوْرِثُ النَّدَامَةَ، وَيَحْبِسُ الرِّزْقَ، وَيَرُدُّ الدُّعَاءَ ❁

﴿٢٧﴾ اَللّٰهُمَّ إِنِّيْ أَسْتَغْفِرُكَ لِكُلِّ ذَنْبٍ مَّدَحْتُهٗ بِلِسَانِيْ، أَوْ أَضْمَرْتُهٗ بِجَنَانِيْ، أَوْ هَشَّتْ إِلَيْهِ نَفْسِيْ، أَوْ أَثْبَتُّهٗ بِلِسَانِيْ، أَوْ أَتَيْتُهٗ بِفِعَالِيْ، أَوْ كَتَبْتُهٗ بِيَدِيْ، أَوِ ارْتَكَبْتُهٗ أَوْ أَرْكَبْتُ فِيْهِ عِبَادَكَ ❁

(28) O Allāh, I seek Your forgiveness for every sin that I committed in solitude during my night and my day, yet You lowered over me a covering so that none besides You—O All-Compelling One—could see me engaged in it. My soul thus fell into confusion, and I wavered between abandoning it out of fear of You and committing it out of good hopes in Your mercy; but my lower self adorned it for me such that I boldly committed it, though being aware that, in doing so, I was disobeying You.

(29) O Allāh, I seek Your forgiveness for every sin that I took to be petty but You took to be grave, that I deemed to be small but You deemed to be great, and in which my own ignorance embroiled me.

(30) O Allāh, I seek Your forgiveness for every sin by which I misguided one of Your creation, or through which I mistreated one of them, or which my lower self made seemingly attractive to me, or which I pointed out to another person, or to which I steered someone besides myself, or in which I intentionally persisted, or to which I remained stubbornly attached out of my foolishness.

(31) O Allāh, I seek Your forgiveness for every sin by which I

﴿٢٨﴾ اَللّٰهُمَّ إِنِّيْ أَسْتَغْفِرُكَ لِكُلِّ ذَنْبٍ خَلَوْتُ بِهٖ فِيْ لَيْلِيْ وَنَهَارِيْ، وَأَرْخَيْتَ فِيْهِ عَلَيَّ السِّتَارَ حَيْثُ لَا يَرَانِيْ فِيْهِ إِلَّا أَنْتَ يَا جَبَّارُ، فَارْتَابَتْ نَفْسِيْ فِيْهِ، وَتَحَيَّرْتُ بَيْنَ تَرْكِيْ لَهٗ بِخَوْفِكَ وَانْتِهَاكِيْ لَهٗ بِحُسْنِ الظَّنِّ فِيْكَ، فَسَوَّلَتْ لِيْ نَفْسِي الْإِقْدَامَ عَلَيْهِ، وَأَنَا عَارِفٌ بِمَعْصِيَتِيْ فِيْهِ لَكَ ۞

﴿٢٩﴾ اَللّٰهُمَّ إِنِّيْ أَسْتَغْفِرُكَ لِكُلِّ ذَنْبٍ اسْتَقْلَلْتُهٗ فَاسْتَعْظَمْتَهٗ، وَاسْتَصْغَرْتُهٗ فَاسْتَكْبَرْتَهٗ، وَوَرَّطَنِيْ فِيْهِ جَهْلِيْ بِهٖ ۞

﴿٣٠﴾ اَللّٰهُمَّ إِنِّيْ أَسْتَغْفِرُكَ لِكُلِّ ذَنْبٍ أَضْلَلْتُ بِهٖ أَحَدًا مِّنْ خَلْقِكَ، أَوْ أَسَأْتُ بِهٖ إِلٰى أَحَدٍ مِّنْ بَرِيَّتِكَ، أَوْ زَيَّنَتْهُ لِيْ نَفْسِيْ، أَوْ أَشَرْتُ بِهٖ إِلٰى غَيْرِيْ، أَوْ دَلَلْتُ عَلَيْهِ سِوَايَ، وَأَصَرَرْتُ عَلَيْهِ بِعَمْدِيْ، أَوْ أَقَمْتُ عَلَيْهِ بِجَهْلِيْ ۞

﴿٣١﴾ اَللّٰهُمَّ إِنِّيْ أَسْتَغْفِرُكَ لِكُلِّ ذَنْبٍ خُنْتُ بِهٖ أَمَانَتِيْ، أَوْ أَحْسَنَتْ

betrayed my trust [of obedience], or whose perpetration my lower self commended to me, or by which I violated the rights of my own body, or in doing which I gave precedence to my base desires over obedience to You, or from which I gained excessive delight, or which I strove to do for the sake of another, or to which I lured my followers, or on which I remained stubborn against one who tried to prevent me, or in committing which I overcame one who tried to obstruct me or subdued him through my cunning, or into which my evil tendencies caused me to slip.

(32) O Allāh, I seek Your forgiveness for every sin for which I employed such cunning that invokes Your wrath, or in committing which I overcame those in Your obedience, or by which I lured—or intended to lure—one of Your creation into disobeying You. And though I made it seem to Your servants that through my endeavors I seek You [and Your pleasure], my true aim was to disobey You, and as such my desire was turned away from Your obedience.

(33) O Allāh, I seek Your forgiveness for every sin that You recorded against me because of my conceit, or ostentation, or desire to be heard, or malice, or rancor, or treachery, or pride, or

لِيْ نَفْسِيْ فِعْلَهُ، أَوْ أَخْطَأْتُ بِهِ عَلٰى بَدَنِيْ، أَوْ قَدَّمْتُ فِيْهِ عَلَيْكَ شَهْوَتِيْ، أَوْ كَثَّرْتُ فِيْهِ لَذَّتِيْ، أَوْ سَعَيْتُ فِيْهِ لِغَيْرِيْ، أَوِ اسْتَغْوَيْتُ إِلَيْهِ مَنْ تَابَعَنِيْ، أَوْ كَابَرْتُ فِيْهِ مَن مَّانَعَنِيْ، أَوْ قَهَرْتُ عَلَيْهِ مَنْ غَلَبَنِيْ، أَوْ غَلَبْتُ عَلَيْهِ بِحِيْلَتِيْ، أَوِ اسْتَزَلَّنِيْ إِلَيْهِ مَيْلِيْ ✿

﴿٣٢﴾ اَللّٰهُمَّ إِنِّيْ أَسْتَغْفِرُكَ لِكُلِّ ذَنْبٍ اسْتَعَنْتُ عَلَيْهِ بِحِيْلَةٍ تُدْنِيْ مِنْ غَضَبِكَ، أَوِ اسْتَظْهَرْتُ بِنَيْلِهِ عَلٰى أَهْلِ طَاعَتِكَ، أَوِ اسْتَلَمْتُ بِهِ أَحَدًا مِّنْ خَلْقِكَ إِلٰى مَعْصِيَتِكَ أَوْ رُمْتُهُ، وَرَأَيْتُ بِهِ عِبَادَكَ أَوْ لَبِسْتُ عَلَيْهِ بِفِعَالِيْ، كَأَنِّيْ بِحِيْلَتِيْ أُرِيْدُكَ، وَالْمُرَادُ بِهِ مَعْصِيَتُكَ، وَالْهَوٰى مُنْصَرِفٌ عَنْ طَاعَتِكَ ✿

﴿٣٣﴾ اَللّٰهُمَّ إِنِّيْ أَسْتَغْفِرُكَ لِكُلِّ ذَنْبٍ كَتَبْتَهُ عَلَيَّ بِسَبَبِ عُجْبٍ كَانَ مِنِّيْ بِنَفْسِيْ، أَوْ رِيَاءٍ أَوْ سُمْعَةٍ أَوْ حِقْدٍ أَوْ شَحْنَاءٍ أَوْ خِيَانَةٍ أَوْ خُيَلَاءَ أَوْ

exultancy, or intemperate mirth, or obstinacy, or envy, or insolence, or ungratefulness, or fervor for other than Your sake, or bigotry, or acquiescence to sin, or blind hope, or extreme avarice, or generous spending for sin, or oppression, or unwarranted cunning, or theft, or lying, or backbiting, or idle amusement, or fruitless talk, or calumny, or useless play, or any such activity that by doing sins are reaped and in pursuing is destruction and grief.

(34) O Allāh, I seek Your forgiveness for every sin in doing which I feared someone besides You, and opposed Your friends, and befriended Your enemies, and forsook those beloved to You, and placed myself in the path of Your anger.

(35) O Allāh, I seek Your forgiveness, through the power You possess over me and over everything, for every sin that I was destined, in Your eternal knowledge, to commit.

(36) O Allāh, I seek Your forgiveness for every sin for which I repented to You, but which I then returned to, breaking the covenant between me and You, out of my insolence and my knowledge of Your abundant forgiveness.

فَرَحٍ أَوْ مَرَحٍ أَوْ عَنَدٍ أَوْ حَسَدٍ أَوْ أَشَرٍ أَوْ بَطَرٍ أَوْ حَمِيَّةٍ أَوْ عَصَبِيَّةٍ أَوْ رِضَاءٍ أَوْ رَجَاءٍ أَوْ شُحٍّ أَوْ سَخَاءٍ أَوْ ظُلْمٍ أَوْ حِيْلَةٍ أَوْ سَرِقَةٍ أَوْ كَذِبٍ أَوْ غِيْبَةٍ أَوْ لَهْوٍ أَوْ لَغْوٍ أَوْ نَمِيْمَةٍ أَوْ لَعْبٍ، أَوْ نَوْعٍ مِّنَ الْأَنْوَاعِ مِمَّا يُكْتَسَبُ بِمِثْلِهِ الذُّنُوْبُ، وَيَكُوْنُ فِيْ اِتِّبَاعِهِ الْعَطَبُ وَالْحُوْبُ ❃

﴿٣٤﴾ اَللّٰهُمَّ إِنِّيْ أَسْتَغْفِرُكَ لِكُلِّ ذَنْبٍ رَّهِبْتُ فِيْهِ سِوَاكَ، وَعَادَيْتُ فِيْهِ أَوْلِيَائَكَ، وَوَالَيْتُ فِيْهِ أَعْدَاءَكَ، وَخَذَلْتُ فِيْهِ أَحِبَّائَكَ، وَتَعَرَّضْتُ لِشَيْءٍ مِّنْ غَضَبِكَ ❃

﴿٣٥﴾ اَللّٰهُمَّ إِنِّيْ أَسْتَغْفِرُكَ لِكُلِّ ذَنْبٍ سَبَقَ فِيْ عِلْمِكَ أَنِّيْ فَاعِلُهُ، بِقُدْرَتِكَ الَّتِيْ قَدَرْتَ بِهَا عَلَيَّ وَعَلٰى كُلِّ شَيْءٍ ❃

﴿٣٦﴾ اَللّٰهُمَّ إِنِّيْ أَسْتَغْفِرُكَ لِكُلِّ ذَنْبٍ تُبْتُ إِلَيْكَ مِنْهُ ثُمَّ عُدتُّ فِيْهِ، وَنَقَضْتُ فِيْهِ الْعَهْدَ فِيْمَا بَيْنِيْ وَبَيْنَكَ جَرَاءَةً مِّنِّيْ عَلَيْكَ لِمَعْرِفَتِيْ بِعَفْوِكَ ❃

(37) O Allāh, I seek Your forgiveness for every sin that has drawn me near to Your punishment, or has distanced me from Your reward, or has hidden from me Your mercy, or has sullied for me Your blessings.

(38) O Allāh, I seek Your forgiveness for every sin by which I—while acquiring some good You had promised—permitted what You had forbidden or forbade what You had permitted. For extreme greed had entered into my heart, and because of it I was deprived of some good that I could have deserved, or by it I deprived another soul of some good that it deserved.

(39) O Allāh, I seek Your forgiveness for every sin that I committed with the good health You granted me, or gained the ability to do because of Your endless blessings, or became more bold in doing due to Your keeping away Your vengeance from me, or toward which I extended my hands by means of Your plentiful sustenance; or any sin that I committed, initially doing some good action seeking therewith Your noble Countenance, but into which my soul's covetousness mixed what invoked Your displeasure.

(40) O Allāh, I seek Your forgiveness for every sin to which my search for excuses and my craving [for the world] invited me, and thus I sought to commit it and so made lawful for myself what You had decreed unlawful.

﴿٣٧﴾ اَللّٰهُمَّ إِنِّيْ أَسْتَغْفِرُكَ مِنْ كُلِّ ذَنْبٍ أَدْنَانِيْ مِنْ عَذَابِكَ، أَوْ أَنْآنِيْ مِنْ ثَوَابِكَ، أَوْ حَجَبَ عَنِّيْ رَحْمَتَكَ، أَوْ كَدَّرَ عَلَيَّ نِعْمَتَكَ ۞

﴿٣٨﴾ اَللّٰهُمَّ إِنِّيْ أَسْتَغْفِرُكَ لِكُلِّ ذَنْبٍ حَلَلْتُ بِهٖ عَقْدًا شَدَدتَّهٗ، أَوْ شَدَدتُّ بِهٖ عَقْدًا حَلَلْتَهٗ بِخَيْرٍ وَّعَدتَّهٗ، فَلَحِقَنِيْ شُحٌّ فِيْ نَفْسِيْ، حُرِمْتُ بِهٖ خَيْرًا أَسْتَحِقُّهٗ أَوْ حَرَمْتُ بِهٖ نَفْسًا تَسْتَحِقُّهٗ ۞

﴿٣٩﴾ اَللّٰهُمَّ إِنِّيْ أَسْتَغْفِرُكَ لِكُلِّ ذَنْبٍ ارْتَكَبْتُهٗ بِشُمُوْلِ عَافِيَتِكَ، أَوْ تَمَكَّنْتُ مِنْهُ بِفَضْلِ نِعْمَتِكَ، أَوْ تَقَوَّيْتُ بِهٖ عَلٰى دَفْعِ نِقْمَتِكَ عَنِّيْ، أَوْ مَدَدتُّ إِلَيْهِ يَدِيْ بِسَابِغِ رِزْقِكَ، أَوْ خَيْرٍ أَرَدتُّ بِهٖ وَجْهَكَ الْكَرِيْمَ، فَخَالَطَنِيْ فِيْهِ شُحُّ نَفْسِيْ بِمَا لَيْسَ فِيْهِ رِضَاكَ ۞

﴿٤٠﴾ اَللّٰهُمَّ إِنِّيْ أَسْتَغْفِرُكَ لِكُلِّ ذَنْبٍ دَعَانِيْ إِلَيْهِ الرُّخَصُ أَوِ الْحِرْصُ، فَرَغِبْتُ فِيْهِ وَحَلَلْتُ لِنَفْسِيْ مَا هُوَ مُحَرَّمٌ عِنْدَكَ ۞

(41) O Allāh, I seek Your forgiveness for every sin that remained hidden from Your creation but did not escape You—for which I repented to You and You forgave me. But I then returned to it, yet You still kept it concealed for me.

(42) O Allāh, I seek Your forgiveness for every sin toward which I walked with my legs, or toward which I extended my hands, or which I closely observed with my eyes, or which I carefully listened to with my ears, or which I uttered with my tongue, or in which I squandered of the sustenance You had provided me. Then, despite my disobedience, I asked You for more sustenance, and You provided it to me. Then again, I used Your sustenance in disobeying You, but You kept Your covering over me. Yet again I asked You for more, and You still did not deprive me. Then after Your increase, I openly transgressed against You, but You did not humiliate me. I have thus constantly persisted in disobeying You, and You have constantly remained clement and benevolent with me—O Most Benevolent of the benevolent!

(43) O Allāh, I seek Your forgiveness for every sin, the minor of which warrants Your painful punishment, the major of which causes Your severe punishment to descend, and the committing of which hastens Your vengeance, and the persisting in which brings an end to Your bounty.

﴿٤١﴾ اَللّٰهُمَّ إِنِّيْ أَسْتَغْفِرُكَ لِكُلِّ ذَنْبٍ خَفِيَ عَلٰى خَلْقِكَ وَلَمْ يَعْزُبْ عَنْكَ، فَاسْتَقَلْتُكَ مِنْهُ فَأَقَلْتَنِيْ، ثُمَّ عُدتُّ فِيْهِ فَسَتَرْتَهُ عَلَيَّ ❁

﴿٤٢﴾ اَللّٰهُمَّ إِنِّيْ أَسْتَغْفِرُكَ لِكُلِّ ذَنْبٍ خَطَوْتُ إِلَيْهِ بِرِجْلِيْ، أَوْ مَدَدتُّ إِلَيْهِ يَدِيْ، أَوْ تَأَمَّلْتُهُ بِبَصَرِيْ، أَوْ أَصْغَيْتُ إِلَيْهِ بِأُذُنِيْ، أَوْ نَطَقْتُ بِهِ بِلِسَانِيْ، أَوْ أَتْلَفْتُ فِيْهِ مَا رَزَقْتَنِيْ، ثُمَّ اسْتَرْزَقْتُكَ عَلٰى عِصْيَانِيْ فَرَزَقْتَنِيْ، ثُمَّ اسْتَعَنْتُ بِرِزْقِكَ عَلٰى عِصْيَانِكَ فَسَتَرْتَ عَلَيَّ، ثُمَّ سَأَلْتُكَ الزِّيَادَةَ فَلَمْ تَحْرِمْنِيْ، ثُمَّ جَاهَرْتُكَ بَعْدَ الزِّيَادَةِ فَلَمْ تَفْضَحْنِيْ، فَلَا أَزَالُ مُصِرًّا عَلٰى مَعْصِيَتِكَ وَلَا تَزَالُ عَائِدًا عَلَيَّ بِحِلْمِكَ وَكَرَمِكَ، يَا أَكْرَمَ الأَكْرَمِيْنَ ❁

﴿٤٣﴾ اَللّٰهُمَّ إِنِّيْ أَسْتَغْفِرُكَ لِكُلِّ ذَنْبٍ يُّوْجِبُ صَغِيْرُهُ أَلِيْمَ عَذَابِكَ، وَيُحِلُّ كَبِيْرُهُ شَدِيْدَ عِقَابِكَ، وَفِيْ إِتْيَانِهِ تَعْجِيْلُ نِقْمَتِكَ، وَفِي الْإِصْرَارِ عَلَيْهِ زَوَالُ نِعْمَتِكَ ❁

(44) O Allāh, I seek Your forgiveness for every sin that nobody knew of but You, and that nobody was aware of but You—it is among those grave sins from which nothing but Your pardon can save me, and which nothing but Your forgiveness and forbearance can encompass.

(45) O Allāh, I seek Your forgiveness for every sin that removes blessings, and causes punishments to descend, and violates the sacred, and prolongs illness, and hastens anguish, and leaves behind it remorse.

(46) O Allāh, I seek Your forgiveness for every sin that obliterates good deeds, and multiplies evil deeds, and causes punishments to descend, and angers You, O Lord of the Heavens!

(47) O Allāh, I seek Your forgiveness for every sin that You are most worthy to forgive, for You were the One most noble in keeping it concealed. Indeed, You are all-worthy of reverent fear and all-worthy of granting forgiveness.

(48) O Allāh, I seek Your forgiveness for every sin by which I wronged one of Your friends while assisting Your enemies and siding with those in Your disobedience against those in Your obedience.

﴿٤٤﴾ اَللّٰهُمَّ إِنِّيْ أَسْتَغْفِرُكَ لِكُلِّ ذَنْبٍ لَّمْ يَطَّلِعْ عَلَيْهِ أَحَدٌ سِوَاكَ، وَلَمْ يَعْلَمْ بِهٖ أَحَدٌ غَيْرُكَ، مِمَّا لَا يُنْجِيْنِيْ مِنْهُ إِلَّا عَفْوُكَ، وَلَا يَسَعُهٗ إِلَّا مَغْفِرَتُكَ وَحِلْمُكَ ❁

﴿٤٥﴾ اَللّٰهُمَّ إِنِّيْ أَسْتَغْفِرُكَ لِكُلِّ ذَنْبٍ يُّزِيْلُ النِّعَمَ، وَيُحِلُّ النِّقَمَ، وَيَهْتِكُ الْحُرَمَ، وَيُطِيْلُ السَّقَمَ، وَيُعَجِّلُ الْأَلَمَ، وَيُوْرِثُ النَّدَمَ ❁

﴿٤٦﴾ اَللّٰهُمَّ إِنِّيْ أَسْتَغْفِرُكَ لِكُلِّ ذَنْبٍ يَّمْحَقُ الْحَسَنَاتِ، وَيُضَاعِفُ السَّيِّئَاتِ، وَيُحِلُّ النَّقِمَاتِ، وَيُغْضِبُكَ، يَا رَبَّ السَّمَاوَاتِ ❁

﴿٤٧﴾ اَللّٰهُمَّ إِنِّيْ أَسْتَغْفِرُكَ لِكُلِّ ذَنْبٍ أَنْتَ أَحَقُّ بِمَغْفِرَتِهٖ إِذْ كُنْتَ أَوْلٰى بِسِتْرِهٖ، فَإِنَّكَ أَهْلُ التَّقْوٰى وَأَهْلُ الْمَغْفِرَةِ ❁

﴿٤٨﴾ اَللّٰهُمَّ إِنِّيْ أَسْتَغْفِرُكَ لِكُلِّ ذَنْبٍ ظَلَمْتُ بِسَبَبِهٖ وَلِيًّا مِّنْ أَوْلِيَائِكَ، مُسَاعَدَةً لِّأَعْدَائِكَ، وَمَيْلًا مَّعَ أَهْلِ مَعْصِيَتِكَ عَلٰى أَهْلِ طَاعَتِكَ ❁

(49) O Allāh, I seek Your forgiveness for every sin in which my deep engrossment cloaked me with humiliation and made me despair of the existence of Your mercy; or it was despair that prevented me from returning to obeying You, as I realized the severity of my crime and mired hopelessly in my low opinion of myself.

(50) O Allāh, I seek Your forgiveness for every sin that would have brought my destruction had it not been for Your forbearance and mercy; and would have entered me into the Abode of Perdition [Hell] had it not been for Your favor; and would have taken me down the path of deviance had it not been for Your guidance.

(51) O Allāh, I seek Your forgiveness for every sin whose perpetration brings loss of hope, and rejection of prayer, and consecutive calamities, and successive anxieties, and multiplied sorrows.

(52) O Allāh, I seek Your forgiveness for every sin that turns my prayer away from You, and prolongs my suffering of Your displeasure, and shortens my hope in You.

﴿٤٩﴾ اَللّٰهُمَّ إِنِّيْ أَسْتَغْفِرُكَ لِكُلِّ ذَنْبٍ أَلْبَسَنِيْ كَثْرَةُ انْهِمَاكِيْ فِيْهِ ذِلَّةً، وَّآيَسَنِيْ مِن وُّجُوْدِ رَحْمَتِكَ، أَوْ قَصُرَ بِي الْيَأْسُ عَنِ الرُّجُوْعِ إِلٰى طَاعَتِكَ، لِمَعْرِفَتِيْ بِعَظِيْمِ جُرْمِيْ وَسُوْءِ ظَنِّيْ بِنَفْسِيْ ❁

﴿٥٠﴾ اَللّٰهُمَّ إِنِّيْ أَسْتَغْفِرُكَ لِكُلِّ ذَنْبٍ أَوْرَثَنِي الْهَلَكَةَ لَوْلَا حِلْمُكَ وَرَحْمَتُكَ، وَأَدْخَلَنِيْ دَارَ الْبَوَارِ لَوْلَا نِعْمَتُكَ، وَسَلَكَ بِيْ سَبِيْلَ الْغَيِّ لَوْلَا إِرْشَادُكَ ❁

﴿٥١﴾ اَللّٰهُمَّ إِنِّيْ أَسْتَغْفِرُكَ لِكُلِّ ذَنْبٍ يَّكُوْنُ فِي اجْتِرَاحِهٖ قَطْعُ الرَّجَاءِ، وَرَدُّ الدُّعَاءِ، وَتَوَاتُرُ الْبَلَاءِ، وَتَرَادُفُ الْهُمُوْمِ، وَتَضَاعُفُ الْغُمُوْمِ ❁

﴿٥٢﴾ اَللّٰهُمَّ إِنِّيْ أَسْتَغْفِرُكَ لِكُلِّ ذَنْبٍ يَّرُدُّ عَنْكَ دُعَائِيْ، وَيُطِيْلُ فِيْ سَخَطِكَ عَنَائِيْ، أَوْ يُقْصِرُ عَنْكَ أَمَلِيْ ❁

(53) O Allāh, I seek Your forgiveness for every sin that kills the heart, and incites anxiety, and preoccupies the mind, and pleases Satan, and angers the All-Merciful.

(54) O Allāh, I seek Your forgiveness for every sin that leaves on its heel despair of Your mercy, and despondency of Your forgiveness, and deprivation of Your vast treasures.

(55) O Allāh, I seek Your forgiveness for every sin for which I despised myself out of reverence for You. I expressed my repentance to You and You accepted it. I invoked Your pardon and You granted it. Then my base desires returned me to my old habits, as I only longed for Your abundant mercy and generous forgiveness, and forgot Your threats [of punishment], and entertained hopes of Your gracious promises [of reward].

(56) O Allāh, I seek Your forgiveness for every sin that will blacken my face on the day when the faces of Your friends will be whitened and the faces of Your enemies will be blackened—when Your enemies will turn, one against another, in reproach, and You will say, "Dispute not with each other in My presence, for I have already sent to you advanced warning" [Qur'ān 50:28].

﴿٥٣﴾ اَللّٰهُمَّ إِنِّي أَسْتَغْفِرُكَ لِكُلِّ ذَنْبٍ يُّمِيْتُ الْقَلْبَ، وَيُشْعِلُ الْكَرْبَ، وَيُشْغِلُ الْفِكْرَ، وَيُرْضِي الشَّيْطَانَ، وَيُسْخِطُ الرَّحْمٰنَ ❁

﴿٥٤﴾ اَللّٰهُمَّ إِنِّيْ أَسْتَغْفِرُكَ لِكُلِّ ذَنْبٍ يُّعَقِّبُ الْيَأْسَ مِن رَّحْمَتِكَ، وَالْقُنُوْطَ مِن مَّغْفِرَتِكَ، وَالْحِرْمَانَ مِنْ سِعَةِ مَا عِنْدَكَ ❁

﴿٥٥﴾ اَللّٰهُمَّ إِنِّيْ أَسْتَغْفِرُكَ لِكُلِّ ذَنْبٍ أَمْقَتُّ عَلَيْهِ نَفْسِيْ إِجْلَالًا لَّكَ، وَأَظْهَرْتُ لَكَ التَّوْبَةَ فَقَبِلْتَ، وَسَأَلْتُكَ الْعَفْوَ فَعَفَوْتَ، ثُمَّ أَعَادَنِي الْهَوٰى إِلٰى مُعَاوَدَتِيْ طَمَعًا فِيْ سِعَةِ رَحْمَتِكَ وَكَرَمِ عَفْوِكَ، نَاسِيًا لِّوَعِيْدِكَ رَاجِيًا لِّجَمِيْلِ وَعْدِكَ ❁

﴿٥٦﴾ اَللّٰهُمَّ إِنِّيْ أَسْتَغْفِرُكَ لِكُلِّ ذَنْبٍ يُّوْرِثُ سَوَادَ الْوَجْهِ يَوْمَ تَبْيَضُّ وُجُوْهُ أَوْلِيَائِكَ وَتَسْوَدُّ وُجُوْهُ أَعْدَائِكَ، إِذَا أَقْبَلَ بَعْضُهُمْ عَلٰى بَعْضٍ يَّتَلَاوَمُوْنَ، فَتَقُوْلُ: لَا تَخْتَصِمُوْا لَدَيَّ وَقَدْ قَدَّمْتُ إِلَيْكُمْ بِالْوَعِيْدِ ❁

(57) O Allāh, I seek Your forgiveness for every sin that I understood to be a sin and, out of shame before You, remained silent when remembering it; and every sin that I concealed in my heart but You knew of in me, for You know what is secret and what is still more hidden.

(58) O Allāh, I seek Your forgiveness for every sin that makes me detestable to Your servants, and repels from me Your friends; or that estranges me to those in Your obedience, due to the disquietude of my disobedience, my mounting grief, and my perpetration of sins.

(59) O Allāh, I seek Your forgiveness for every sin that calls to unbelief, and prolongs indecisiveness in thought, and leads to poverty, and brings on hardship, and prevents prosperity, and rends the covering from over my sins, and prevents ease.

(60) O Allāh, I seek Your forgiveness for every sin that draws nearer [to people] their appointed times of death, and severs hopes [in Your mercy], and spoils good deeds.

﴿٥٧﴾ اَللّٰهُمَّ إِنِّيْ أَسْتَغْفِرُكَ لِكُلِّ ذَنْبٍ فَهِمْتُهُ، وَصَمَتُّ عَنْهُ حَيَاءً مِّنْكَ عِنْدَ ذِكْرِهِ، أَوْ كَتَمْتُهُ فِيْ صَدْرِيْ وَعَلِمْتَهُ مِنِّيْ، فَإِنَّكَ تَعْلَمُ السِّرَّ وَأَخْفٰى ❁

﴿٥٨﴾ اَللّٰهُمَّ إِنِّيْ أَسْتَغْفِرُكَ لِكُلِّ ذَنْبٍ يُّبْغِضُنِيْ إِلٰى عِبَادِكَ، وَيُنَفِّرُ عَنِّيْ أَوْلِيَائَكَ، أَوْ يُوْحِشُنِيْ مِنْ أَهْلِ طَاعَتِكَ، بِوَحْشَةِ الْمَعَاصِيْ وَرُكُوبِ الْحُوْبِ، وَارْتِكَابِ الذُّنُوْبِ ❁

﴿٥٩﴾ اَللّٰهُمَّ إِنِّيْ أَسْتَغْفِرُكَ لِكُلِّ ذَنْبٍ يَّدْعُوْ إِلَى الْكُفْرِ، وَيُطِيْلُ الْفِكْرَ، وَيُوْرِثُ الْفَقْرَ، وَيَجْلِبُ الْعُسْرَ، وَيَصُدُّ عَنِ الْخَيْرِ، وَيَهْتِكُ السِّتْرَ، وَيَمْنَعُ الْيُسْرَ ❁

﴿٦٠﴾ اَللّٰهُمَّ إِنِّيْ أَسْتَغْفِرُكَ لِكُلِّ ذَنْبٍ يُّدْنِي الْآجَالَ، وَيَقْطَعُ الْآمَالَ، وَيَشِيْنُ الْأَعْمَالَ ❁

(61) O Allāh, I seek Your forgiveness for every sin that pollutes what You have made pure, and exposes of me what You have covered [of my wrongdoings], or makes repulsive what You have beautified in me.

(62) O Allāh, I seek Your forgiveness for every sin because of which Your promise cannot be obtained, and in the presence of which safety from Your wrath cannot be felt, Your mercy cannot descend, and Your permanent favors cannot be attained.

(63) O Allāh, I seek Your forgiveness for every sin in doing which I concealed myself from Your servants in the light of day but openly and daringly opposed You by committing in the darkness of night. This I did while knowing that secrets are open to You, and that the hidden is exposed to You, and that nothing can protect me from Your punishment, nor can anything—neither my wealth nor my children—avail me before You, except that I come to You with a sound heart.

(64) O Allāh, I seek Your forgiveness for every sin that causes forgetfulness of Your remembrance; or that brings on its heel heedlessness of Your warning and drives me to senselessly feel safe from Your devising; or that causes me to despair of the good reward You possess.

﴿٦١﴾ اَللّٰهُمَّ إِنِّيْ أَسْتَغْفِرُكَ لِكُلِّ ذَنْبٍ يُّدَنِّسُ مَا طَهَّرْتَهُ، وَيَكْشِفُ عَنِّيْ مَا سَتَرْتَهُ، أَوْ يُقَبِّحُ مِنِّيْ مَا زَيَّنْتَهُ ❀

﴿٦٢﴾ اَللّٰهُمَّ إِنِّيْ أَسْتَغْفِرُكَ لِكُلِّ ذَنْبٍ لَّا يُنَالُ بِهِ عَهْدُكَ، وَلَا يُؤْمَنُ مَعَهُ غَضَبُكَ، وَلَا تَنْزِلُ بِهِ رَحْمَتُكَ، وَلَا تَدُوْمُ مَعِيْ نِعْمَتُكَ ❀

﴿٦٣﴾ اَللّٰهُمَّ إِنِّيْ أَسْتَغْفِرُكَ لِكُلِّ ذَنْبِ اسْتَخْفَيْتُ بِهِ فِيْ ضَوْءِ النَّهَارِ عَنْ عِبَادِكَ، وَبَارَزْتُكَ بِهِ فِيْ ظُلْمَةِ اللَّيْلِ جَرَاءَةً مِّنِّيْ عَلَيْكَ، عَلٰى أَنِّيْ أَعْلَمُ أَنَّ السِّرَّ عِنْدَكَ عَلَانِيَةٌ، وَّأَنَّ الْخَفِيَّةَ عِنْدَكَ بَارِزَةٌ، وَّأَنَّهُ لَا يَمْنَعُنِيْ مِنْكَ مَانِعٌ، وَّلَا يَنْفَعُنِيْ عِنْدَكَ نَافِعٌ مِّن مَّالٍ وَّبَنِيْنَ، إِلَّا أَنْ أَتَيْتُكَ بِقَلْبٍ سَلِيْمٍ ❀

﴿٦٤﴾ اَللّٰهُمَّ إِنِّيْ أَسْتَغْفِرُكَ لِكُلِّ ذَنْبٍ يُّوْرِثُ النِّسْيَانَ لِذِكْرِكَ، أَوْ يُعَقِّبُ الْغَفْلَةَ عَنْ تَحْذِيْرِكَ، وَيَتَمَادٰى بِيْ إِلَى الْأَمْنِ مِن مَّكْرِكَ، أَوْ يُؤَيِّسُنِيْ مِنْ خَيْرِ مَا عِنْدَكَ ❀

(65) O Allāh, I seek Your forgiveness for every sin that overtook me because I disrespectfully complained and objected to You for withholding Your subsistence from me, and because I turned away from You and inclined instead toward Your [powerless] servants in submissiveness and earnest petition; whereas You had let me hear Your clear statement in Your Book, "But they humbled not themselves to their Lord, nor did they submissively entreat [Him]" [Qur'ān 23:76].

(66) O Allāh, I seek Your forgiveness for every sin that remained with me because, when anxiety struck, I sought aid, succor, and support from someone besides You.

(67) O Allāh, I seek Your forgiveness for every sin to which fear of someone besides You drove me, and it [the fear] called me to earnestly entreat one of Your creation or inclined me to yearn for what others besides You possessed—so I preferred to obey them and disobey You in order to lay hand on what they had, though I was aware that I am in need of You and that I am never free and independent of Your support.

﴿٦٥﴾ اَللّٰهُمَّ إِنِّيْ أَسْتَغْفِرُكَ لِكُلِّ ذَنْبٍ لَّحِقَنِيْ بِسَبَبِ عَتْبِيْ عَلَيْكَ فِيْ إِحْبَاسِ الرِّزْقِ عَلَيَّ، وَشِكَايَتِيْ مِنْكَ، وَإِعْرَاضِيْ عَنْكَ، وَمَيْلِيْ إِلٰى عِبَادِكَ بِالْاِسْتِكَانَةِ لَهُمْ وَالتَّضَرُّعِ إِلَيْهِمْ، وَقَدْ أَسْمَعْتَنِيْ قَوْلَكَ فِيْ مُحْكَمِ كِتَابِكَ: فَمَا اسْتَكَانُوْا لِرَبِّهِمْ وَمَا يَتَضَرَّعُوْنَ ❁

﴿٦٦﴾ اَللّٰهُمَّ إِنِّيْ أَسْتَغْفِرُكَ لِكُلِّ ذَنْبٍ لَّزِمَنِيْ بِسَبَبِ كُرْبَةٍ اسْتَغَثْتُ عِنْدَهَا بِغَيْرِكَ، وَاسْتَعَنْتُ عَلَيْهَا بِسِوَاكَ، وَاسْتَمْدَدتُّ بِأَحَدٍ فِيْهَا دُوْنَكَ ❁

﴿٦٧﴾ اَللّٰهُمَّ إِنِّيْ أَسْتَغْفِرُكَ لِكُلِّ ذَنْبٍ حَمَلَنِيْ عَلَيْهِ الْخَوْفُ مِنْ غَيْرِكَ، وَدَعَانِيْ إِلَى التَّضَرُّعِ لِأَحَدٍ مِّنْ خَلْقِكَ، أَوِ اسْتَمَالَنِيْ إِلَى الطَّمَعِ فِيْمَا عِنْدَ غَيْرِكَ، فَآثَرْتُ طَاعَتَهُ فِيْ مَعْصِيَتِكَ اسْتِجْلَابًا لِّمَا فِيْ يَدَيْهِ، وَأَنَا أَعْلَمُ بِحَاجَتِيْ إِلَيْكَ كَمَا لَا غِنٰى لِيْ عَنْكَ ❁

(68) O Allāh, I seek Your forgiveness for every sin that my soul made seem to me trivial and small, and continued to make seem insignificant, until it finally entangled me in it.

(69) O Allāh, I seek Your forgiveness for every sin that Your pen recorded and Your knowledge encompassed—every one that I have committed and that I am to commit until the end of my life. I seek Your forgiveness for all my sins: the first and the last, the intentional and the unintentional, the few and the many, the minor and the major, the subtle and the noticeable, the past and the recent, the secret and the open and public—and all those I am to commit throughout my life.

(70) O Allāh, I seek Your forgiveness for every sin of mine. I ask You to forgive me all the injustices against Your servants that You have enumerated against me; for Your servants have against me many claims of violated rights and injustices to which I am held captive. O Allāh, even if these evil deeds of mine are many in number, they are a paltry few in sight of Your forgiveness. O Allāh, any male or female servant of Yours who has against me a claim of injustice, that I forcibly seized from him something

﴿٦٨﴾ اَللّٰهُمَّ إِنِّيْ أَسْتَغْفِرُكَ لِكُلِّ ذَنْبٍ مَثَّلَتْ لِيْ نَفْسِي اسْتِقْلَالَهُ، وَصَوَّرَتْ لِي اسْتِصْغَارَهُ، وَقَلَّلَتْهُ حَتّٰى وَرَّطَتْنِيْ فِيْهِ ✿

﴿٦٩﴾ اَللّٰهُمَّ إِنِّيْ أَسْتَغْفِرُكَ لِكُلِّ ذَنْبٍ جَرٰى بِهِ قَلَمُكَ، وَأَحَاطَ بِهِ عِلْمُكَ فِيَّ وَعَلَيَّ إِلٰى آخِرِ عُمْرِيْ، وَلِجَمِيْعِ ذُنُوْبِيْ كُلِّهَا، أَوَّلِهَا وَآخِرِهَا، عَمْدِهَا وَخَطَئِهَا، قَلِيْلِهَا وَكَثِيْرِهَا، صَغِيْرِهَا وَكَبِيْرِهَا، دَقِيْقِهَا وَجَلِيْلِهَا، قَدِيْمِهَا وَحَدِيْثِهَا، سِرِّهَا وَجَهْرِهَا وَعَلَانِيَتِهَا، وَلِمَا أَنَا مُذْنِبٌ فِيْ جَمِيْعِ عُمْرِيْ ✿

﴿٧٠﴾ اَللّٰهُمَّ إِنِّيْ أَسْتَغْفِرُكَ لِكُلِّ ذَنْبٍ لِّيْ، وَأَسْأَلُكَ أَنْ تَغْفِرَ لِيْ مَا أَحْصَيْتَ عَلَيَّ مِن مَّظَالِمِ الْعِبَادِ قِبَلِيْ، فَإِنَّ لِعِبَادِكَ عَلَيَّ حُقُوْقًا وَّمَظَالِمَ وأَنَا بِهَا مُرْتَهِنٌ، اَللّٰهُمَّ وَإِنْ كَانَتْ كَثِيْرَةً فَإِنَّهَا فِيْ جَنْبِ عَفْوِكَ يَسِيْرَةٌ، اللّٰهُمَّ أَيُّمَا عَبْدٍ مِّنْ عِبَادِكَ أَوْ أَمَةٍ مِّنْ إِمَائِكَ كَانَتْ لَهُ مَظْلِمَةٌ عِنْدِيْ، قَدْ غَصَبْتُهُ، عَلَيْهَا فِيْ أَرْضِهِ أَوْ مَالِهِ أَوْ عِرْضِهِ أَوْ بَدَنِهِ، أَوْ غَابَ

of his land or wealth or honor or body—whether he was absent or present, or whether he or his representatives demanded from me compensation for it but neither was I able to return it to him nor did I seek to be pardoned for it—I ask that You, with Your benevolence, generosity, and abundant treasures, satisfy them on my behalf; and do not give them over me power to take away and decrease my good deeds. For indeed, You possess what can satisfy them on my behalf, and I do not. And do not make a way for their bad deeds to overcome my good deeds on the Day of Judgment.

[CONCLUDING PRAYERS]

I seek forgiveness from Allāh—besides Whom there is nothing worthy of worship—the Living, the Self-Subsisting Sustainer of all creation. And I turn to Him seeking forgiveness that increases one hundred million times with every blink of the eye and with every breath, that remains as long as Allāh remains and lasts as long as Allāh lasts; for His Dominion will never—for all of eternity—come to an end, cease, or die away. O Allāh, accept this prayer.

O Allāh, make mine a prayer that meets with Your acceptance and a request that meets with Your blessing. Indeed You have power over all things.

أَوْ حَضَرَ هُوَ أَوْ خَصْمُهُ يُطَالِبُنِي بِهَا، وَلَمْ أَسْتَطِعْ أَنْ أَرُدَّهَا إِلَيْهِ وَلَمْ أَسْتَحْلِلْهَا مِنْهُ، فَأَسْأَلُكَ بِكَرَمِكَ وَجُوْدِكَ وَسِعَةِ مَا عِنْدَكَ، أَنْ تُرْضِيَهُمْ عَنِّيْ، وَلَا تَجْعَلَ لَهُمْ عَلَيَّ شَيْئًا مُّنَقِّصَةً مِّنْ حَسَنَاتِيْ، فَإِنَّ عِنْدَكَ مَا يُرْضِيْهِمْ عَنِّيْ وَلَيْسَ عِنْدِيْ مَا يُرْضِيْهِمْ، وَلَا تَجْعَلْ يَوْمَ الْقِيَامَةِ لِسَيِّئَاتِهِمْ عَلَىٰ حَسَنَاتِيْ سَبِيْلًا ❁

أَسْتَغْفِرُ اللهَ الَّذِيْ لَا إِلٰهَ إِلَّا هُوَ الْحَيُّ الْقَيُّوْمُ وَأَتُوْبُ إِلَيْهِ، اسْتِغْفَارًا يَّزِيْدُ فِيْ كُلِّ طَرْفَةِ عَيْنٍ وَّتَحْرِيْكَةِ نَفْسٍ مِّائَةَ أَلْفِ أَلْفِ ضِعْفٍ، يَّدُوْمُ مَعَ دَوَامِ اللهِ وَيَبْقٰى مَعَ بَقَاءِ اللهِ، الَّذِيْ لَا فَنَاءَ وَلَا زَوَالَ وَانْتِقَالَ لِمُلْكِهِۦ، أَبَدَ الْآبِدِيْنَ وَدَهْرَ الدَّاهِرِيْنَ، سَرْمَدًا فِيْ سَرْمَدٍ، اسْتَجِبْ بِاللهِ ❁

اَللّٰهُمَّ اجْعَلْ دُعَاءً وَّافَقَ إِجَابَةً، وَّمَسْأَلَةً وَّافَقَتْ مِنْكَ عَطِيَّةً، إِنَّكَ عَلٰى كُلِّ شَيْءٍ قَدِيْرٌ ❁

O Allāh, send blessings on our Master Muḥammad, and upon the family of our Master Muḥammad, and upon his Companions; and grant them abundant peace. Grant them abundant blessings and peace that remain as long as You remain and last as long as You last, that have bounds only You can know—blessings that please You and him, and by which You are pleased with us, O Lord of the worlds! And for this, all praise is due to Allāh.

Glory to your Lord, the Lord of All-Eminence, [who is far above] what they claim. And peace be upon all the Messengers. And all Praise is due to Allāh, the Lord and Cherisher of the Worlds.

[CONCLUDING NOTES]

[ʿAllāma Quṭb al-Dīn states:] "Here end 'the prayers for forgiveness that save from the Hellfire,' attributed to Ḥasan al-Baṣrī. I have quoted them from numerous editions. I also came across one edition of these prayers, at the beginning of which was mentioned that they had been related from our master, the leader of the faithful, ʿAlī [ibn Abī Ṭālib] (may Allāh ennoble his face and be pleased with him), and that he would recite them in the latter part of each night. It has been related that the latter part of the night until the rise of dawn

اَللّٰهُمَّ صَلِّ عَلٰى سَيِّدِنَا مُحَمَّدٍ وَّعَلٰى آلِ سَيِّدِنَا مُحَمَّدٍ وَّصَحْبِهٖ وَسَلِّمْ تَسْلِيْمًا كَثِيْرًا، صَلَاةً دَائِمَةً بِدَوَامِكَ بَاقِيَةً بِبَقَائِكَ، لَا مُنْتَهٰى لَهَا دُوْنَ عِلْمِكَ، صَلَاةً تُرْضِيْكَ وَتُرْضِيْهِ وَتَرْضٰى بِهَا عَنَّا، يَا رَبَّ الْعَالَمِيْنَ، وَسَلِّمْ كَذٰلِكَ، وَالْحَمْدُ لِلّٰهِ عَلٰى ذٰلِكَ ❁

سُبْحَانَ رَبِّكَ رَبِّ الْعِزَّةِ عَمَّا يَصِفُوْنَ، وَسَلَامٌ عَلَى الْمُرْسَلِيْنَ، وَالْحَمْدُ لِلّٰهِ رَبِّ الْعَالَمِيْنَ ❁

is the most superior time for invoking Allāh for forgiveness. Also, in many narrations, it is mentioned that the most complete formula for seeking forgiveness is to do so seventy times.

I ask from all the believers who come across these prayers and benefit from them, that they not forget me in their good prayers and that they seek forgiveness for me. [The translator and publisher requests the same.] We hope from Allāh that He forgive us all."

Transliteration

1. Allāhumma innī astaghfiruka li kulli dhambin qawiya ʿalayhi badanī bi ʿāfiyatik(a), wa nālat-hu qudratī bi faḍli niʿmatik(a), wa 'mbasaṭat ilayhi yadī bi si-ʿati rizqik(a), wa 'ḥtajabtu ʿani 'n-nāsi bi sitrik(a), wa 'ttakaltu fīhi ʿinda khawfī minka ʿalā amānik(a), wa wathiqtu min saṭwatika ʿalayya fīhi bi ḥilmik(a), wa ʿawwaltu fīhi ʿalā karami wajhika wa ʿafwik(a). Fa ṣalli yā Rabbi wa sallim wa bārik ʿalā Sayyidinā Muḥammad(iw), wa ʿalā āli Sayyidinā Muḥammad(iw), wa 'ghfirhu lī yā Khayra 'l-ghāfirīn(a).

2. Allāhumma innī astaghfiruka li kulli dhambiy yadʿū ilā ghaḍabik(a), aw yudnī min sakhaṭik(a), aw yamīlu bī ilā mā nahaytanī ʿanh(u), aw yubā-ʿidunī ʿammā da-ʿawtanī ilayh(i).

3. Allāhumma innī astaghfiruka li kulli dhambin aslamtu ilayhi aḥadam min khalqika bi ghawāyatī, aw khadaʿtuhū bi ḥīlatī, fa ʿallamtuhū minhu mā jahil(a), wa zayyantu lahū mā qad ʿalim(a), wa laqītuka ghadam bi awzārī wa awzārim ma-ʿa awzārī.

4. Allāhumma innī astaghfiruka li kulli dhambiy yadʿū ila 'l-ghay-

y(i), wa yuḍillu ʿani 'r-rushd(i), wa yuqillu 'l-wafr(a), wa yamḥaqu 't-tālida(ta), wa yukhmilu 'dh-dhikr(a), wa yuqillu 'l-ʿadad(a).

5. Allāhumma innī astaghfiruka li kulli dhambin atʿabtu fīhi jawāriḥī fī laylī wa nahārī, wa qadi 'statartu ḥayā'am min ʿibādika bi sitrik(a), wa lā sitra illā mā satartanī bih(ī).

6. Allāhumma innī astaghfiruka li kulli dhambin qaṣadanī bihī aʿdā'ī li hatkī, fa ṣarafta kaydahum ʿannī, wa lam tu-ʿinhum ʿalā faḍīḥatī ka'annī laka muṭī-ʿ(uw), wa naṣartanī ḥattā ka'annī laka waliyy(un). Wa ilā matā, yā Rabbi, aʿṣī fa tumhilunī? Wa ṭālamā ʿaṣaytuka fa lam tu'ākhidhnī, wa sa'altuka ʿalā sū'i fiʿlī fa aʿṭaytanī, fa ayyu shukriy yaqūmu ʿindaka bi niʿmatim min ni-ʿamika ʿalayy(a).

7. Allāhumma innī astaghfiruka li kulli dhambin qaddamtu ilayka tawbatī minh(u), wa wājahtuka bi qasamī bik(a), wa ashhattu ʿalā nafsī bi dhālika awliyā'aka min ʿibādika anni ghayru ʿā'idin ilā maʿṣiyatik(a), fa lammā qaṣadanī ilayhi bi kaydihi 'sh-shayṭān(u), wa māla bī ilayhi 'l-khudhlān(u), wa da-ʿatnī nafsī ila 'l-ʿiṣyan(i), istatartu ḥayā'am min ʿibadika jarā'atam minnī ʿalayk(a), wa ana aʿlamu annahū lā yukinnunī minka sitruw wa lā bāb(uw), wa lā yaḥjubu naẓaraka ḥijāb(un), fa khālaftuka fi 'l-maʿṣiyati ilā mā nahaytanī ʿanh(u), thumma mā kashafta 's-sitr(a), wa sāwaytanī bi awliyā'ik(a), ka'anni lā azālu laka muṭī-ʿaw, wa ilā amrika musri-ʿaw, wa min wa-ʿīdika fāzi-ʿan, fa labistu ʿalā ʿibadik(a), wa lā yaʿlamu sarīratī ghayruk(a), fa lam tasimnī bi ghayri simatihim, bal asbaghta ʿalayya mithla niʿmatihim, thumma faḍḍaltanī bi dhālika ʿalayhim ka'annī

ᶜindaka fī darajatihim, wa mā dhāka illā li ḥilmika wa faḍli niᶜmatika faḍlam minka ᶜalayy(a). Fa laka 'l-ḥamdu yā Mawlāy(a). Fa as'aluka yā Allāhu kamā satartahū ᶜalayya fi 'd-dunyā, allā tafḍaḥanī bihī yawma 'l-qiyāmati, yā Arḥama 'r-rāḥimīn(a).

8. Allāhumma innī astaghfiruka li kulli dhambin sahirtu fīhi laylatī fī ladhdhatī, fi 't-ta'annī li ityānihī wa 't-takhalluṣi ilā wujūdihī wa taḥṣīlih(ī), ḥattā idhā aṣbaḥtu ḥaḍartu ilayka bi ḥilyati 'ṣ-ṣāliḥīn(a), wa ana muḍmirun khilāfa riḍāka, yā Rabba 'l-ᶜālamīn(a).

9. Allāhumma innī astaghfiruka li kulli dhambin ẓalamtu bi sababihī waliyyam min awliyā'ik(a), wa naṣartu bihī ᶜaduwwam min aᶜdā'ik(a), aw takallamtu fīhi li ghayri maḥabbatik(a), aw nahaḍtu fīhi ilā ghayri ṭā-ᶜatik(a), aw dhahabtu fīhi ilā ghayri amrik(a).

10. Allāhumma innī astaghfiruka li kulli dhambiy yūrithu 'ḍ-ḍaghnā'(a), wa yuḥillu 'l-balā'(a), wa yushmitu 'l-aᶜdā'(a), wa yak-shifu 'l-ghiṭā'(a), wa yaḥbisu 'l-qaṭra mina 's-samā'(i).

11. Allāhumma innī astaghfiruka li kulli dhambin alhānī ᶜammā hadaytanī ilayh(i), wa amartanī bihī aw nahaytanī ᶜanh(u), aw dalaltanī ᶜalayhi mimmā fīhi 'l-ḥaẓẓu lī, wa 'l-bulūghu ilā riḍāka wa 'ttibā-ᶜu maḥabbatika wa īthāru 'l-qurbi mink(a).

12. Allāhumma innī astaghfiruka li kulli dhambin nasītuhū fa aḥṣaytah(ū), wa tahāwantu bihī fa athbattah(ū), wa jāhartuka bihī fa satartahū ᶜalayy(a), wa law tubtu ilayka minhu la ghafartah(ū).

13. Allāhumma innī astaghfiruka li kulli dhambin tawaqqaᶜtu minka

qabla 'nqiḍā'ihī taʿjīla 'l-ʿuqūba(ti), fa amhaltanī wa asbalta ʿalayya sitran, fa lam ālu fī hatkihī ʿannī juhdan.

14. Allāhumma innī astaghfiruka li kulli dhambin nahaytanī ʿanhu fa khālaftuka ilayh(i), wa ḥadhdhartanī iyyāhu fa aqamtu ʿalayh(i), wa qabbaḥtahū ʿalayya fa zayyanat-hu lī nafsī.

15. Allāhumma innī astaghfiruka li kulli dhambiy yaṣrifu ʿannī raḥmatak(a), aw yuḥillu bī niqmatak(a), aw yaḥrimunī karāmatak(a), aw yuzīlu ʿannī niʿmatak(a).

16. Allāhumma innī astaghfiruka li kulli dhambin ʿayyartu bihī aḥadam min khalqik(a), aw qabbaḥtu min fiʿli aḥadim mim bariyyatik(a), thumma taqaḥḥamtu ʿalayhi wa 'ntahaktuhū jarā'atam minnī ʿalayk(a).

17. Allāhumma innī astaghfiruka li kulli dhambin tubtu ilayka minhu wa aqdamtu ʿalā fiʿlih(ī), fa 'staḥyaytu minka wa ana ʿalayh(i), wa rahibtuka wa ana fīh(i), thumma 'staqaltuka minhu wa ʿuttu ilayh(i).

18. Allāhumma innī astaghfiruka li kulli dhambin tawarraka ʿalayya wa wajaba fī shay'in fa-ʿaltuhū bi sababi ʿahdin ʿahittuka ʿalayh(i), aw ʿaqdin ʿaqattuhū lak(a), aw dhimmatin ālaytu bihā min ajlika li aḥadim min khalqik(a), thumma naqaḍtu dhālika min ghayri ḍarūratil lazimatnī fīh(i), bali 'stanzalanī ʿani 'l-wafā'i bihi 'l-baṭar(u), wa as-khaṭanī ʿar ri-ʿāyatihi 'l-ashar(u).

19. Allāhumma innī astaghfiruka li kulli dhambil laḥiqanī bi sababi

niʿmatin anʿamta bihā ʿalayy(a), fa taqawwaytu bihā ʿalā ma-ʿāṣīk(a), wa khālaftu fīhā amrak(a), wa aqdamtu bihā ʿalā wa-ʿīdik(a).

20. Allāhumma innī astaghfiruka li kulli dhambin qaddamtu fīhi shahwatī ʿalā ṭā-ʿatik(a), wa āthartu fīhi maḥabbatī ʿalā amrik(a), fa arḍaytu nafsī bi ghaḍabik(a), wa ʿarrattuhā li sakhaṭik(a), idh nahaytanī wa qaddamta ilayya fīhi indhāraka wa taḥajjajta ʿalayya fīhi bi wa-ʿīdik(a), wa astaghfiruka 'Llāhumma wa atūbu ilayk(a).

21. Allāhumma innī astaghfiruka li kulli dhambin ʿalimtuhu min nafsī fa ansaytuhū aw dhakartuh(ū), aw ta-ʿammattuhū aw akhṭa'tu fīh(i), wa huwa mimmā lā ashukku annaka musā'ilī ʿanh(u), wa anna nafsī bihī murtahinatul ladayk(a), wa in kuntu qad nasītuhū wa ghafalat ʿanhu nafsī.

22. Allāhumma innī astaghfiruka li kulli dhambiw wājahtuka fīhi wa qad ayqantu annaka tarānī ʿalayh(i), fa nawaytu an atūba ilayka minh(u), wa unsītu an astaghfiraka minh(u), ansānīhi 'sh-shayṭān(u).

23. Allāhumma innī astaghfiruka li kulli dhambin dakhaltu fīhi bi ḥusni ẓannī fīka annaka lā tu-ʿadhdhibunī ʿalayh(i), wa rajawtuka li maghfiratihī fa aqdamtu ʿalayh(i), wa qad ʿawwaltu nafsī ʿalā maʿrifatī bi karamika allā tafḍaḥanī bihī baʿda idh satartahū ʿalayy(a).

24. Allāhumma innī astaghfiruka li kulli dhambini 'stawjabtu bihī minka radda 'd-du-ʿā'(i), wa ḥirmāna 'l-ijābati wa khaybata 'ṭ-ṭamaʿ(i), wa 'inqiṭā-ʿa 'r-rajā'(i).

25. Allāhumma innī astaghfiruka li kulli dhambiy yūrithu 'l-asqāma wa 'ḍ-ḍinā, wa yūjibu 'n-niqama wa 'l-balā'(a), wa yakūnu yawma 'l-qiyamati ḥasrataw wa nadāma(tan).

26. Allāhumma innī astaghfiruka li kulli dhambiy yu-ᶜaqqibu 'l-ḥasra(ta), wa yūrithu 'n-nadāma(ta), wa yaḥbisu 'r-rizq(a), wa yaruddu 'd-du-ᶜā'(a).

27. Allāhumma innī astaghfiruka li kulli dhambim madaḥtuhū bi lisānī, aw aḍmartuhū bi janānī, aw hashshat ilayhi nafsī, aw athbattuhū bi lisānī, aw ataytuhū bi fi-ᶜālī, aw katabtuhū bi yadī, awi 'rtakabtuhū aw arkabtu fīhi ᶜibādak(a).

28. Allāhumma innī astaghfiruka li kulli dhambin khalawtu bihī fī laylī wa nahārī, wa arkhayta fīhi ᶜalayya 's-sitāra ḥaythu lā yarānī fīhi illā anta yā Jabbār(u), fa 'rtābat nafsī fīh(i), wa taḥayyartu bayna tarkī lahū bi khawfika wa 'ntihākī lahū bi ḥusni 'ẓ-ẓanni fīk(a), fa sawwalat lī nafsi 'l-iqdāma ᶜalayh(i), wa ana ᶜārifun bi maᶜṣiyatī fīhi lak(a).

29. Allāhumma innī astaghfiruka li kulli dhambini 'staqlaltuhū fa 'staᶜẓamtah(ū), wa 'staṣghartuhū fa 'stakbartah(ū), wa warraṭanī fīhi jahlī bih(ī).

30. Allāhumma innī astaghfiruka li kulli dhambin aḍlaltu bihī aḥadam min khalqik(a), aw asa'tu bihī ilā aḥadim mim bariyyatik(a), aw zayyanat-hu lī nafsī, aw ashartu bihī ilā ghayrī, aw dalaltu ᶜalayhi siwāy(a), wa aṣrartu ᶜalayhi bi ᶜamdī, aw aqamtu ᶜalayhi bi jahlī.

31. Allāhumma innī astaghfiruka li kulli dhambin khuntu bihī

amānatī, aw aḥsanat lī nafsī fiʿlah(ū), aw akhṭa'tu bihī ʿalā badanī, aw qaddamtu fīhi ʿalayka shahwatī, aw kaththartu fīhi ladhdhatī, aw saʿaytu fīhi li ghayrī, awi 'staghwaytu ilayhi man tāba-ʿanī, aw kābartu fīhi mam māna-ʿanī, aw qahartu ʿalayhi man ghalabanī, aw ghalabtu ʿalayhi bi ḥīlatī, awi 'staẓallanī ilayhi maylī.

32. Allāhumma innī astaghfiruka li kulli dhambini 'sta-ʿantu ʿalayhi bi ḥīlatin tudnī min ghaḍabik(a), awi 'staẓhartu bi naylihī ʿalā ahli ṭā-ʿatik(a), awi 'stalamtu bihī aḥadam min khalqika ilā maʿṣiyatika aw rumtuh(ū), wa ra'aytu bihī ʿibādaka aw labistu ʿalayhi bi fi-ʿālī ka'annī bi ḥīlatī urīduk(a), wa 'l-murādu bihī maʿṣiyatuk(a), wa 'l-hawā munṣarifun ʿan ṭā-ʿatik(a).

33. Allāhumma innī astaghfiruka li kulli dhambin katabtahū ʿalayya bi sababi ʿujbin kāna minnī bi nafsī, aw riyā'in, aw sum-ʿatin, aw ḥiqdin, aw shaḥnā'in, aw khiyānatin, aw khuyalā'a, aw faraḥin, aw maraḥin, aw ʿanadin, aw ḥasadin, aw asharin, aw baṭarin, aw ḥamiyyatin, aw ʿaṣabiyyatin, aw riḍā'in, aw rajā'in, aw shuḥḥin, aw sakhā'in, aw ẓulmin, aw ḥīlatin, aw sariqatin, aw kadhibin, aw ghībatin, aw lahwin, aw laghwin, aw namīmatin, aw laʿbin, aw naw-ʿim mina 'l-anwā-ʿi mimma yuktasabu bi mithlihi 'dh-dhunūb(u), wa yakūnu fi 'ttibā-ʿihi 'l-ʿaṭabu wa 'l-ḥūb(u).

34. Allāhumma innī astaghfiruka li kulli dhambir rahibtu fīhi siwāk(a), wa ʿādaytu fīhi awliyā'ak(a), wa wālaytu fīhi aʿdā'ak(a), wa khadhaltu fīhi aḥibbā'ak(a), wa ta-ʿarraḍtu li shay'im min ghaḍabik(a).

35. Allāhumma innī astaghfiruka li kulli dhambin sabaqa fī ʿilmika annī fā-ʿiluhū bi qudratika 'llatī qadarta bihā ʿalayya wa ʿalā kulli shay'(in).

36. Allāhumma innī astaghfiruka li kulli dhambin tubtu ilayka minhu thumma ʿuttu fīh(i), wa naqaḍtu fīhi 'l-ʿahda fīmā baynī wa baynaka jarā'atam minnī ʿalayka li maʿrifatī bi ʿafwik(a).

37. Allāhumma innī astaghfiruka li kulli dhambin adnānī min ʿadhābik(a), aw an'ānī min thawābik(a), aw ḥajaba ʿannī raḥmatak(a), aw kaddara ʿalayya niʿmatak(a).

38. Allāhumma innī astaghfiruka li kulli dhambin ḥalaltu bihī ʿaqdan shadattah(ū), aw shadattu bihī ʿaqdan ḥalaltahū bi khayriw wa-ʿattah(ū), fa laḥiqanī shuḥḥun fī nafsī, ḥurimtu bihī khayran astaḥiqquhū aw ḥaramtu bihī nafsan tastaḥiqquh(ū).

39. Allāhumma innī astaghfiruka li kulli dhambini 'rtakabtuhū bi shumūli ʿāfiyatik(a), aw tamakkantu minhu bi faḍli niʿmatik(a), aw taqawwaytu bihī ʿalā daf-ʿi niqmatika ʿannī, aw madattu ilayhi yadī bi sābighi rizqik(a), aw khayrin arattu bihī wajhaka 'l-karīm(a), fa khālaṭanī fīhi shuḥḥu nafsī bi mā laysa fīhi riḍāk(a).

40. Allāhumma innī astaghfiruka li kulli dhambin da-ʿānī ilayhi 'r-rukhaṣu awi 'l-ḥirṣ(u), fa raghibtu fīhi wa ḥalaltu li nafsī mā huwa muḥarramun ʿindak(a).

41. Allāhumma innī astaghfiruka li kulli dhambin khafiya ʿalā khal-

qika wa lam yaᶜzub ᶜank(a), fa 'staqaltuka minhu fa aqaltanī, thumma ᶜuttu fīhi fa satartahū ᶜalayy(a).

42. Allāhumma innī astaghfiruka li kulli dhambin khaṭawtu ilayhi bi rijlī, aw madattu ilayhi yadī, aw ta'ammaltuhū bi baṣarī, aw aṣghaytu ilayhi bi udhunī, aw naṭaqtu bihī bi lisānī, aw atlaftu fīhi mā razaqtanī, thumma 'starzaqtuka ᶜalā ᶜiṣyānī fa razaqtanī, thumma 'sta-ᶜantu bi rizqika ᶜalā ᶜiṣyānika fa satarta ᶜalayy(a), thumma sa'altuka 'z-ziyadata fa lam taḥrimnī, thumma jāhartuka baᶜda 'z-ziyādati fa lam tafḍaḥnī, fa lā azālu muṣirran ᶜalā maᶜṣiyatika wa lā tazālu ᶜā'idan ᶜalayya bi ḥilmika wa karamika, yā Akrama 'l-akramīn(a).

43. Allāhumma innī astaghfiruka li kulli dhambiy yūjibu ṣaghīruhū alīma ᶜadhābik(a), wa yuḥillu kabīruhū shadīda ᶜiqābik(a), wa fī ityānihī taᶜjīlu niqmatik(a), wa fī 'l-iṣrāri ᶜalayhi zawālu niᶜmatik(a).

44. Allāhumma innī astaghfiruka li kulli dhambil lam yaṭṭaliᶜ ᶜalayhi aḥadun siwāk(a), wa lam yaᶜlam bihī aḥadun ghayruk(a), mimmā lā yunjīnī minhu illā ᶜafwuk(a), wa lā yasa-ᶜuhū illā maghfiratuka wa ḥilmuk(a).

45. Allāhumma innī astaghfiruka li kulli dhambiy yuzīlu 'n-niᶜam(a), wa yuḥillu 'n-niqam(a), wa yahtiku 'l-ḥaram(a), wa yuṭīlu 's-saqam(a), wa yu-ᶜajjilu 'l-alam(a), wa yūrithu 'n-nadam(a).

46. Allāhumma innī astaghfiruka li kulli dhambiy yamḥaqu 'l-ḥasanāt(i), wa yuḍā-ᶜifu 's-sayyi'āt(i), wa yuḥillu 'n-naqamāt(i), wa yughḍibuka yā Rabba 's-samāwāt(i).

47. Allāhumma innī astaghfiruka li kulli dhambin anta aḥaqqu bi maghfiratihī idh kunta awlā bi sitrih(ī), fa innaka Ahlu 't-taqwā wa Ahlu 'l-maghfira(ti).

48. Allāhumma innī astaghfiruka li kulli dhambin ẓalamtu bi sababihī waliyyam min awliyā'ika musā-ᶜadatal li aᶜdā'ik(a), wa may-lam ma-ᶜa ahli maᶜṣiyatika ᶜalā ahli ṭā-ᶜatik(a).

49. Allāhumma innī astaghfiruka li kulli dhambin albasanī kathratu inhimākī fīhi dhilla(taw), wa āyasanī min wujūdi raḥmatik(a), aw qaṣura bī 'l-ya'su ᶜani 'r-rujūᶜi ilā ṭā-ᶜatik(a), li maᶜrifatī bi ᶜaẓīmi jurmī wa sū'i ẓannī bi nafsī.

50. Allāhumma innī astaghfiruka li kulli dhambin awrathani 'l-hala-kata law lā ḥilmuka wa raḥmatuk(a), wa adkhalanī dāra 'l-bawāri law lā niᶜmatuk(a), wa salaka bī sabīla 'l-ghayyi law lā irshāduk(a).

51. Allāhumma innī astaghfiruka li kulli dhambiy yakūnu fi 'jtirāḥihī qatᶜu 'r-rajā'(i), wa raddu 'd-du-ᶜā'(i), wa tawāturu 'l-balā'(i), wa tarādufu 'l-humūm(i), wa taḍā-ᶜufu 'l-ghumūm(i).

52. Allāhumma innī astaghfiruka li kulli dhambiy yaruddu ᶜanka du-ᶜā'ī, wa yuṭīlu fī sakhaṭika ᶜanā'ī, aw yuqṣiru ᶜanka amalī.

53. Allāhumma innī astaghfiruka li kulli dhambiy yumītu 'l-qalb(a), wa yushᶜilu 'l-karb(a), wa yushghilu 'l-fikr(a), wa yurḍī 'sh-shay-ṭān(a), wa yus-khiṭu 'r-Raḥmān(a).

54. Allāhumma innī astaghfiruka li kulli dhambiy yu-ᶜaqqibu 'l-ya'sa

mir raḥmatik(a), wa 'l-qunūṭa mim maghfiratik(a), wa 'l-ḥirmāna min si-ʿati mā ʿindak(a).

55. Allāhumma innī astaghfiruka li kulli dhambin amqattu ʿalayhi nafsī ijlālal lak(a), wa aẓhartu laka 't-tawbata fa qabilt(a), wa sa'altuka 'l-ʿafwa fa ʿafawt(a), thumma a-ʿādanī 'l-hawā ilā mu-ʿāwadatī ṭama-ʿan fī si-ʿati raḥmatika wa karami ʿafwik(a), nāsiyal li wa-ʿīdika rājiyal li jamīli waʿdik(a).

56. Allāhumma innī astaghfiruka li kulli dhambiy yūrithu sawāda 'l-wajhi yawma tabyaḍḍu wujūhu awliyā'ika wa taswaddu wujūhu aʿdā'ik(a), idh aqbala baʿḍuhum ʿalā baʿḍiy yatalāwamūn(a), fa taqūl(u): lā takhtaṣimū ladayya wa qad qaddamtu ilaykum bi 'l-wa-ʿīd(i).

57. Allāhumma innī astaghfiruka li kulli dhambin fahimtuh(ū), wa ṣamattu ʿanhu ḥayā'am minka ʿinda dhikrih(ī), aw katamtuhū fī ṣadrī wa ʿalimtahū minnī, fa innaka taʿlamu 's-sirra wa akhfā.

58. Allāhumma innī astaghfiruka li kulli dhambiy yubghiḍunī ilā ʿibādik(a), wa yunaffiru ʿannī awliyā'ak(a), aw yūḥi-shunī min ahli ṭā-ʿatik(a), bi waḥshati 'l-ma-ʿāṣī wa rukūbi 'l-ḥūbi wa 'rtikābi 'dh-dhunūb(i).

59. Allāhumma innī astaghfiruka li kulli dhambiy yad-ʿū ilā 'l-kuf-r(i), wa yuṭīlu 'l-fikr(a), wa yūrithu 'l-faqr(a), wa yajlibu 'l-ʿusr(a), wa yaṣuddu ʿani 'l-khayr(i), wa yahtiku 's-sitr(a), wa yamna-ʿu 'l-yusr(a).

60. Allāhumma innī astaghfiruka li kulli dhambiy yudni 'l-ājāl(a), wa yaqṭa-ʿu 'l-āmāl(a), wa yashīnu 'l-aʿmāl(a).

61. Allāhumma innī astaghfiruka li kulli dhambiy yudannisu mā ṭahhartah(ū), wa yakshifu ʿannī mā satartah(ū), aw yuqabbiḥu minnī mā zayyantah(ū).

62. Allāhumma innī astaghfiruka li kulli dhambil lā yunālu bihī ʿahduk(a), wa lā yu'manu maʿahū ghaḍabuk(a), wa lā tanzilu bihī raḥmatuk(a), wa lā tadūmu ma-ʿī niʿmatuk(a).

63. Allāhumma innī astaghfiruka li kulli dhambini 'stakhfaytu bihī fī ḍaw'i 'n-nahāri ʿan ʿibādik(a), wa bāraztuka bihī fī ẓulmati 'l-layli jarā'atam minnī ʿalayk(a), ʿalā annī aʿlamu anna 's-sirra ʿindaka ʿalāniya(tun), wa anna 'l-khafiyyata ʿindaka bāriza(tun), wa annahū lā yamna-ʿunī minka māni-ʿ(un), wa lā yanfa-ʿunī ʿindaka nāfi-ʿum mim māliw wa banīn(a), illā an ataytuka bi qalbin salīm(in).

64. Allāhumma innī astaghfiruka li kulli dhambiy yūrithu 'n-nisyāna li dhikrik(a), aw yu-ʿaqqibu 'l-ghaflata ʿan taḥdhīrik(a), wa yatamādā bī ila 'l-amni mim makrik(a), aw yu'ayyisunī min khayri mā ʿindak(a).

65. Allāhumma innī astaghfiruka li kulli dhambil laḥiqanī bi sababi ʿatbī ʿalayka fī iḥbāsi 'r-rizqi ʿalayy(a), wa shikāyatī mink(a), wa iʿrāḍī ʿank(a), wa maylī ilā ʿibādika bi 'l-istikānati lahum, wa 't-taḍarru-ʿi ilayhim, wa qad asmaʿtanī qawlaka fī muḥkami kitābik(a): fama 'stakānū li Rabbihim wa mā yataḍarra-ʿūn(a).

66. Allāhumma innī astaghfiruka li kulli dhambil lazimanī bi sababi kurbatini 'sta-ghathtu ʿindahā bi ghayrik(a), wa 'sta-ʿantu ʿalayhā bi siwāk(a), wa 'stamdattu bi aḥadin fīhā dūnak(a).

67. Allāhumma innī astaghfiruka li kulli dhambin ḥamalanī ʿalayhi 'l-khawfu min ghayrik(a), wa da-ʿānī ila 't-taḍarru-ʿi li aḥadim min khalqik(a), awi 'stamālanī ila 'ṭ-ṭama-ʿi fīmā ʿinda ghayrik(a), fa āthartu ṭā-ʿatahū fī maʿṣiyatika 'stijlābal limā fī yadayh(i), wa ana aʿlamu bi ḥājatī ilayka kamā lā ghinā lī ʿank(a).

68. Allāhumma innī astaghfiruka li kulli dhambim maththalat lī nafsi 'stiqlālah(ū), wa ṣawwarat li 'stiṣghārah(ū), wa qallalat-hu ḥattā warraṭatnī fīh(i).

69. Allāhumma innī astaghfiruka li kulli dhambin jarā bihī qalamuk(a), wa aḥāṭa bihī ʿilmuka fīyya wa ʿalayya ilā ākhiri ʿumrī, wa li jamī-ʿi dhunūbī kullihā, awwalihā wa ākhirihā, ʿamdihā wa khaṭa'ihā, qalīlihā wa kathīrihā, ṣaghīrihā wa kabīrihā, daqīqihā wa jalīlihā, qadīmihā wa ḥadīthihā, sirrihā wa jahrihā wa ʿalāniyatihā, wa limā ana mudhnibun fī jamī-ʿi ʿūmrī.

70. Allāhumma innī astaghfiruka li kulli dhambil lī, wa as'aluka an taghfira lī mā aḥṣayta ʿalayya min maẓālimi 'l-ʿibādi qibalī, fa inna li ʿibādika ʿalayya ḥuqūqan wa maẓālima wa ana bihā murtahin(un). Allāhumma wa in kānat kathīratan fa innahā fī jambi ʿafwika yasīra(tun). Allāhumma ayyumā ʿabdim min ʿibādika aw amatim min imā'ika kānat lahū maẓlimatun ʿindī, qad ghaṣabtuhū ʿalayhā fī arḍihī aw mālihī aw ʿirḍihī aw badanih(ī), aw ghāba aw ḥaḍara huwa

aw khaṣmuhū yuṭālibunī bihā wa lam astaṭiᶜ an aruddahā ilayhi wa lam astaḥlilhā minh(u), fa as'aluka bi karamika wa jūdika wa si-ᶜati mā ᶜindak(a), an turḍiyahum ᶜannī, wa lā taj-ᶜal lahum ᶜalayya shay'am munaqqiṣatam min ḥasanātī, fa inna ᶜindaka mā yurḍīhim, wa laysa ᶜindī mā yurḍīhim, wa lā tajᶜal yawma 'l-qiyāmati li sayyi'ātihim ᶜalā ḥasanātī sabīlan.

Astaghfiru 'Llāha 'lladhī lā ilāha illā Huwa 'l-Ḥayyu 'l-Qayyūmu wa atūbu ilayh(i), 'stighfāray yazīdu fī kulli ṭarfati ᶜayniw wa taḥrīkati nafsim mi'ata alfi alfi ḍiᶜf(iy), yadūmu ma-ᶜa dawāmi 'Llāhi wa yabqā ma-ᶜa baqā'i 'Llāh(i), 'lladhī lā fanā'a wa lā zawāla wa 'ntiqāla li mulkih(ī), abada 'l-ābidīna wa dahra 'd-dāhirīn(a), sarmadan fī sarmad(in), istajib bi 'Llāh(i).

Allāhumma 'jᶜal du-ᶜā'aw wāfaqa ijāba(taw), wa mas'alataw wāfaqat minka ᶜaṭiyya(tan), innaka ᶜalā kulli shay'in qadīr(un).

Allāhumma ṣalli ᶜalā Sayyidinā Muḥammadiw wa ᶜalā āli Sayyidinā Muḥammadiw wa ṣaḥbihī wa sallim taslīman kathīran, ṣalātan dā'imatam bi dawāmika bāqiyatam bi baqā'ik(a), lā muntahā lahā dūna ᶜilmik(a), ṣalātan turḍīka wa turḍīhi wa tarḍā bihā annā, ya Rabba 'l-ᶜālamīn(a), wa sallim kadhālik(a), wa 'l-ḥamdu li 'Llāhi alā dhālik(a).

Subḥāna Rabbika Rabbi 'l-ᶜizzati ᶜammā yaṣifūn(a), wa salāmun ᶜala 'l-mursalīn(a), wa 'l-ḥamdu li 'Llāhi Rabbi 'l-ᶜālamīn(a).

سند الاستغفارات المنقذة من النار

Chain of Transmission of the Prayers for Forgiveness that Save from the Hellfire

ʿAllāma Quṭb al-Dīn al-Ḥanafī (may Allāh Most High have mercy on him) states in his book *Prayers of Ḥajj and ʿUmra:* "When the night of Tarwiya, the seventh night of Dhū 'l-Ḥijja, arrives, one should recite the *'Prayers of Forgiveness that Save from the Hellfire'* attributed to Ḥasan al-Baṣrī (may Allāh be pleased with him)—during this night. Those whom Allāh has guided toward good fortune (*saʿāda*) from among His special friends and righteous servants recite this punctually. My father Shaykh ʿAlā' al-Dīn (may Allāh have mercy on him) used to recite them regularly.

I relate these prayers from him through my transmission from his teacher, the ḥadīth master of the world, the illuminating sun of the community and religion, Muḥammad ibn ʿAbd al-Raḥmān al-Sakhāwī (may Allāh have mercy on him); [who relates] from [two people,] the Shaykh, Ascetic, and Sufi, Abū 'l-ʿAbbās Aḥmad ibn Muḥammad al-ʿAqabī, and from the virtuous and righteous lady, remnant of the early generations, Umm Muḥammad Zaynab bint ʿAbdillāh al-ʿIrbānī. The former [Abū 'l-ʿAbbās] says, "The righteous female scholar Umm ʿĪsā Maryam bint al-Shāb Aḥmad ibn Muḥammad ibn Ibrāhīm al-Adhruʿī al-Ḥanafī informed us;" and the latter [Umm Muḥammad] says, "Al-Shihāb Aḥmad ibn al-Najm Ayyūb ibn Ibrāhīm al-Qarāfī, who was known as Ibn al-Munaffar and was a pious man, informed us—who then both narrate from Abū 'l-Ḥasan ʿAlī ibn ʿUmar ibn Abī Bakr al-Wānī al-Ṣūfī, [only that] the second narrator adds that she heard the narration directly from him; that we were informed by Abū 'l-Qāsim ʿAbd al-Raḥmān

قال العلامة الشيخ قُطْب الدين الحنفي رحمه الله تعالى في كتابه: أدعية الحج والعمرة: وإذا كانت ليلة التَّرْوِيَة، وهي ليلة سبع من ذي الحجة، قرأ الاستغفارات المنقذة من النار المنسوبة إلى الحسن رضي الله عنه في هذه الليلة يواظب عليها من وفقه الله للسعادة من خِلْص أولياءه وعباده الصالحين، وكان يواظب عليها والدي الشيخ علاءُ الدين رحمه الله تعالى.

وأنا أرويها عنه بروايتي عن أستاذه حافظ الدنيا شمس الملة والدين محمد بن عبد الرحمن السَّخَاوِي رحمه الله تعالى عن الشيخ الزاهد الصوفي أبي العباس أحمدَ بنِ محمد العَقَبِي، والخيرة الصالحة بقية السلف أمُّ محمدٍ زينبُ ابنة عبدِ الله العِرْبَانِي، قال الأول: أنبأتنا الشيخةُ الصالحة أمُّ عيسى مريمُ ابنة الشاب أحمدُ بن محمد بن إبراهيم الأَذْرُعِي الحنفي، قالت الأخرى: أخبرنا الشهابُ أحمدُ بن النجم أيوب بن إبراهيم القَرَافِي الشهير بابن المنفر وكان صالحًا، كلاهما عن أبي الحسن عليٍّ بن عمر بن أبي بكر الوَانِي الصوفي (قال ثانيهما سماعًا)، أنبأَنَا أبو القاسم عبدُ الرحمن بن مكي الطَرَابُلُسِي الصوفي قالا: أنبأَنَا الحافظ أبو طاهر أحمدُ بن محمد السِّلَفي الصوفي أنبأَنَا أبو عبد الله أحمدُ بن علي الأَسْوَاني الصوفي بأَصْبَهَانَ أنبأَنَا أبو الحسن عليُّ بن شجاع بن محمد الشَيْبَاني المَصْقَلِي في المُذَكِّرِ أنبأَنَا أبو علي أحمدُ بن عثمانَ الزَيْدي الصوفي عن جُنَيْد البَغْدَادي عن سَرِيٍّ السَّقَطِي عن معروف الكَرْخِي أنبأَنَا معبد بن عبد العزيز العابد عن الحسن البصري رضي الله عنه:

ibn Makkī al-Ṭarabulūsī al-Ṣūfī; they say that we were informed by Abū Ṭāhir Aḥmad ibn Muḥammad al-Silafī al-Ṣūfī, who says we were informed by Abū ʿAbdillah Aḥmad ibn ʿAlī al-Aswānī al-Ṣūfī, in Isfahan, who says we were informed by Abū al-Ḥasan ʿAlī ibn Shujāʿ ibn Muḥammad al-Shaybānī al-Maṣqalī, during his admonition, that we were informed by Abū ʿAlī Aḥmad ibn ʿUthmān al-Zaydī al-Ṣūfī, from Junayd al-Baghdādī from Sarī al-Saqaṭī from Maʿrūf al-Karkhī, who said we were informed by Maʿbad ibn ʿAbd al-ʿAzīz al-ʿĀbid from Ḥasan al-Baṣrī (may Allāh be pleased with him) who says:

I had always wished to see a friend or dear servant of Allāh, either while awake or in a dream, so that I could ask him of a need of mine, until one year, while I was standing in ʿArafāt at noon, I suddenly noticed eight people by the Arāk [trees] in the environs of the Valley of Nuʿmān facing the Mount of the Valley of Ṣakharāt. I resolved that they were the ones I was seeking, so I approached them and greeted them, to which they responded most cordially. Among them was an elderly man whose face Allāh had illuminated and its brilliance was ascending to the horizon. I sat with them and felt little in myself when I observed the calmness and tranquility they possessed in them. Then one of them stood up, made the call for prayer, and then made the call to commence. At this the elderly man proceeded forth and led them in prayer. I prayed with them, and I knew that there was no prayer—nor would there be any—recorded in my book

(قال) كنت أتمنى أن أرى في عمري وليًّا من أولياء الله تعالى أو صديقًا فأسأله عن حاجتي في اليقظة أو في المنام حتى إذا كانت سنة من السنين وأنا واقف بعرفات عند الزوال وإذا بثمانية أنفس عند الأراك الذي بحيال وادي نُعْمَانَ نحو جبل وادي الصخرات فتحققت أنهم القوم فقصدتهم وسلّمت عليهم فردّوا عليّ أحسن رد وإذا فيهم شيخ كبير قد نوّر الله وجهه فعلا نوره الأفق فجلست معهم وقد تصاغرت نفسي عندي لما شاهدت فيهم من الوقار والسكينة فقام أحدهم فأذَّن وأقام فتقدم الشيخ فصلى بهم، فصليت معهم وأَنَا أعلم أنه ما كُتِب في صحيفتي مثلها ولا يكتب ثم استقبل القبلة بعد الصلاة فقال: الحمد لله كثيرًا، فلم أسمع غيرها وخفت أن يفوتوني أو يغيبوا عني، فقلت للذي يليني بحق الذي اصطفاك بِمَ نلت هذه المنزلة وهذه الفضيلة؟ قال: فتغير وجهه وفتح عينيه فقال له الشيخ: من يهدي الله فهو المهتدي اهدِه يرحمك الله، فقال: كنت أقول: الاستغفار المنقذ من النار في ثلاث ليال، فقلت: ما هذا الاستغفار؟ وما هذه الليالي؟ فقال: ليلة سبع من ذي الحجة وليلة تسع وليلة عشر ولو علم قائلها ما يقول وبأي شيء يتلفظ لكان حقاً على الله أن يرزقه الأمن يوم الفزع الأكبر، ويخصه بالرحمة والولاية، فقلت: علِّمْنيها يرحمك الله تعالى، فقال لي: هي هذه:

of deeds with a value like this one. After the prayer, he faced in the direction of the Kaʿba and then said: "For Allāh is abundant praise." I did not hear him say anything other than that. I feared that my opportunity to be with them [and benefit from them] would pass, or that they would soon take leave of me, so I said to the one next to me, "By Allāh, the One Who has chosen you, how have you achieved this [great] status and [moral] excellence?" His face changed, and he opened his eyes [in surprise], upon which the elderly man said to him, "Whomever Allāh guides, he is truly guided. Show him the way; may Allāh have mercy on you." So the one besides me said to me, "I used to recite the *'Prayers of Forgiveness that Save from the Hellfire'* during three nights." I asked as to exactly what these prayers were and in which nights they were recited? He said, "[I recite them on] the nights of the seventh, ninth and tenth of Dhū 'l-Ḥijja, and if the one reciting them really knows what he is reciting and what words he is uttering, it is incumbent upon Allāh to provide him with security on the day of great grief [Judgment Day], and to distinguish him with [His] mercy and friendship." I said, "Teach me these prayers; may Allāh Most High have mercy on you." So he said to me,

They are [...].

ʿAllāma Quṭb al-Dīn al-Ḥanafī

Quṭb al-Dīn al-Ḥanafī (may Allāh have mercy on him) is Muḥammad ibn Aḥmad ibn Muḥammad ibn Qā.dī Khān ibn Yāʿqūb al-ʿAdanī al-Kharqānī al-Qādarī; his agnomen is Abū ʿĪsā, and he is popularly known as al-Naharwālī and al-Quṭb al-Makkī. With ancestry from Gujarat, India, he was born in 917 A.H. (1511 C.E.) in Lahore and became an inhabitant of the noble city of Makka, where he spent most of his life.

He held the office of Muftī (expert on legal opinion) of Makka. He was a jurist, Qur'ānic commentator, ḥadīth master (*ḥāfiẓ*), poet, an outstanding scholar of Arabic language, literature, history, and the transmitted and logical sciences, and he was one of the foremost Ḥanafī scholars of his time. Among his students were the renowned Mullā ʿAlī al-Qārī and ʿAbd al-Ḥaq al-Sanbāṭī.

He studied under his father, Shaykh ʿAlā' al-Dīn, and under Shaykh Muḥammad al-Tūnisī, Nāṣir al-Dīn al-Laqānī, Aḥmad ibn Yūnus al-Shalabī, Jamāl al-Dīn Ḥirbāqī, and the Yemeni ḥadīth scholar (*muḥaddith*) Abū Muḥammad ʿAbd al-Raḥmān ibn ʿAlī al-

Shaybānī al-ʿAbdarī al-Zabīdī. In 943 AH, he traveled to Egypt and studied under Abū ʿAbdillāh Muḥammad ibn Yaʿqūb al-ʿAbbāsī al-Mutawakkil ʿala Allāh (d. 950 AH) and under some students of Jalāl al-Dīn al-Suyūṭī. He took the spiritual path (*ṭarīqa*) from Shaykh ʿAlā al-Dīn al-Kirmānī al-Naqshabandī (d. 939 AH). He also traveled twice to Istanbul for knowledge, after which he returned to Makka.

He related the *Ṣaḥīḥ* of Imām Abū Ismaʿil al-Bukhārī through one of the shortest known chains, comprising only eight links between him and the great Imām. Among his written works are *Tarīkh al-Kaʿba al-Musharrafa* (History of the Noble Kaʿba), *Al-Iʿlām bi Aʿlām Baytillāh al-Ḥarām* (The Guide to the Luminaries of the Noble House of Allāh), and *Ṭabaqāt al-Ḥanafiyya* (Degrees of the Ḥanafī Jurists)—the third was destroyed in a fire among some other of his works.

He was held in high esteem by the Ottoman Turks, and with the stipends received from them, he would purchase useful and precious books and distribute them among those in need of them. He died on Saturday 27 Rabīʿ al-Thānī 990 A.H. (1582 C.E.), or 991 A.H. (1583 C.E.), during the morning call to prayer.

Adapted from the forthcoming publication Balad Allāh al-Ḥarām wa Aʿlām al-Ḥanafiyya al-Kirām, by Shaykh Ahmad ibn Muhammad Bagia.

Bibliography

ʿAbd al-Majīd, Muḥammad Ḥanīf. *Istighfār kī sattar duʿāin.* Karachi, Pakistan: Zam Zam Publishers.

ʿAlī, Abdullāh Yūsuf. *The Holy Qur'ān: English Translation of the Meanings & Commentary.* Revised and Edited by the Presidency of Islamic Researches, Iftā, Call & Guidance. Madīnah Munawwara, Saudi Arabia: King Fahd Holy Qur'ān Printing Press.

Hammad, Ahmad Zaki. *The Gracious Quran: An English Interpretation of Its Meanings.* United States of America: Straight Angle, Inc.

Ibn Manẓūr, *Lisān al-ʿArab.* Third edition. Beirut, Lebanon: Dār Iḥyā' al-Turāth al-ʿArabī and Mu'assasa al-Tarīkh al-ʿArabī.

Lane, E. W. *Arabic-English Lexicon.* Cambridge, England: Islamic Text -Society.

Naharwālī, Quṭb al-Dīn al-Ḥanafī, *Kitāb Adʿiyat al-Ḥajj wa 'l-ʿUmra* [printed at the end of Ḥusayn ibn Ṣaʿīd ʿAbd al-Ghanī al-Makkī al-Ḥanafī's *Irshād al-sārī ilā Manāsik al-Mullā ʿAlī al-Qārī*]. Beirut, Lebanon: Dār al-Kitāb al-ʿArabī.

Nuʿmānī, Muḥammad Manẓūr. *Maʿārif al-Ḥadīth.* Lahore, Pakistan: ʿUmar Fārūq Academy.

Wehr, Hans. *A Dictionary of Modern Written Arabic.* Edited by J. Milton Cowan. Beirut, Lebanon: Librarie Du Liban.